AIRBUS A310

AIRLIFE'S AIRLINERS 10

AIRBUS A310

Günter Endres

Airlife
England

First published in the UK in 2000
by Airlife Publishing Ltd

British Library Cataloguing-in-Publication Data
A catalogue record for this book
is available from the British Library

ISBN 1 85310 958 4

Printed in Singapore by Kyodo Printing Co (S'pore) Pte Ltd

Airlife Publishing Ltd
101 Longden Road, Shrewsbury, SY3 9EB, England
E-mail: airlife@airlifebooks.com
Website: www.airlifebooks.com

PREVIOUS PAGE: The first extended-range A310-300 with Pratt & Whitney JT9D-7R4E engines Pratt & Whitney-powered A310-300 skims over runway on a low fly-past during its maiden flight. *All photographs in the book, unless otherwise credited, are courtesy Airbus Industrie*

BELOW: The A310 is on its final approach. Unless military orders are forthcoming, the order book is likely to remain closed.

CONTENTS

INTRODUCTION

The European Airbus is a success story by any criteria. Having taken international co-operation to a new level, against the odds and in the face of much scepticism from both sides of the Atlantic, Airbus Industrie is today challenging the mighty Boeing for leadership in the manufacture of civil airliners. How effective this challenge has been can be gauged by the fact that from a standing start in the early 1970s, Airbus now has carved out for itself a near equal marketshare with its US competitor, and continues to go from strength to strength.

It certainly was not an easy process, and there were moments in its history when the future looked decidedly bleak. Britain's wavering attitude, which shifted from the enthusiastic to a complete pull-out in 1969 (before re-committing itself to the programme 10 years later) was not helpful, and French nationalistic fervour also once brought Airbus to the edge. But all these early problems were overcome by men of vision from all participating countries, who were able to see beyond cultural differences and national squabbles, to the long-term benefit such co-operation would bring.

It had long become clear that individual manufacturers could no longer finance the huge development costs of large aircraft, especially as government funds and support were begin-

BELOW: Cyprus Airways A310-200.

ning to dry up as demand on the public purse increased. The risk of letting the industry wither was that Europe's flag-carriers would be left with no choice but to buy US aircraft, giving the likes of Boeing, McDonnell Douglas and Lockheed free rein over the commercial aircraft market. Co-operation on joint programmes was the only answer if Europe's manufacturers were not to be relegated to becoming little more than subcontractors to their US counterparts.

The result of Britain, France, Germany, the Netherlands and Spain working together for the good of Europe and their own countries' manufacturing industries in an increasingly competitive environment are here for all to see. As we move into a new millennium, the Airbus order book stands at more than 3,500 aircraft from 170 customers right across the world. While the single-aisle A320 family has taken the bulk of the orders, the long-range A330/A340 models are also winning the argument against competing aircraft, and will be followed by still larger and longer-legged models, including most likely the double-deck 600-seat A3XX.

But it is to the A310, and the A300 from which it is derived, the credit must go for laying the foundation for a family of aircraft ranging in size from 100 seats to 440 seats, and everything in between. The A300/A310 models have logged

close to 800 orders, of which the A310 accounts for 261 units. While in terms of quantity, the A310 may be viewed as the least successful of the Airbus models, it deserves its place in history through introducing the latest technological advances and providing the link into the digital age.

The A310 undoubtedly benefited from the hard-earned success of the larger A300, but it can be argued that it should have been the first Airbus model to be built. It appeared to be the right size required by all the targeted airlines (except Air France), but in the end the French carrier won the argument and the A300B10, as it was then referred to, was put on the backburner. It took 10 years, and much lobbying by some of Europe's leading airlines headed by Lufthansa and Swissair, before the smaller A310 took its rightful place alongside its big brother. A new aircraft family was born.

Günter Endres
Lindfield, West Sussex

Acknowledgements

Having previously written about the A300 (volume 8 of Airlife's Airliners series), much of the research had also included the A310, since there was much commonality, especially with the later A300-600/600R variants. The knowledge gained from the A300 made it slightly easier to prepare a similar volume on the smaller aircraft, yet could still not have been achieved without the help and assistance of many friends, acquaintances and organisations.

I was fortunate to visit Airbus Industrie in Toulouse, where I was able to search through press releases, printed material and extensive photo files. This would not, however, have been possible without the kind assistance from the ever-present Barbara Kracht, whose father had also played such a pivotal role in Airbus, and David Velupillai, who worked wonders in balancing his extensive workload with my frequent demands. Bernard Ziegler, who as chief test pilot took the A310 to the air for the first time in April 1982, was kind enough to impart his in-depth knowledge of the aircraft. There were many others at Airbus who gave their time and made an invaluable contribution to the book.

Many a gap in facts and figures, photographs and airline operations were plugged through the invaluable help of a number of people, some of whom I have known for a long time. Others among a dwindling band of enthusiasts have become familiar through their own published contributions to the knowledge of aviation history and were kind enough to assist. Among these are Mike Stroud, Ricky-Dene Halliday, Lothar Müller, Carsten Jorgensen, Luis Rosa, Terry Shone, Patrick McDermott, Jefferson Luis Melchioretto and Omar Zekria.

I again managed to persuade my friends Dave Carter and Graham Humberstone, both airline captains, to plough through my manuscript and help me to avoid embarrassing howlers, especially in the area of technical specifications and descriptions. It takes some time to read 30,000 words and check against flight and training manuals and I am indebted to them. My sincere gratitude also goes to those, albeit far too few airlines, which put in the effort to provide current and historic information.

BELOW: A310-300 prototype noses up to the Aerospatiale facilities in Toulouse.

ABOVE: Transavia A310-300. *Patrick McDermott*

BELOW: Spanish carrier Air Plus Comet operates the A310-300 on charter flights in
Europe and to the Americas. *Luis Rosa*

1 BACKGROUND AND EVOLUTION

The A310 was the second member of what is now an extended and still growing family of Airbus aircraft. Many in the industry still believe that it should have been built ahead of the A300, as several airlines expressed their conviction at the time that a smaller 200-seat widebody twin, optimised for short stage lengths, was the way to go. Although the smaller family member had always been an option during the development of the Airbus product, it took some 10 years before it finally came to fruition, due largely to the persistence of Lufthansa and Swissair, which had both been early proponents of the type. But the idea of building a European airliner from scratch — first mooted in the early 1960s — was a momentous step beyond previous limited collaborations between manufacturers on either side of the English Channel. Selecting exactly the right product required much careful deliberation and consultation. However, before delving into the development of the aircraft, a brief review of the difficult birth of the Airbus consortium will help to build the framework which made the A310 possible.

For the first decades after World War II, and as a result of it, European aircraft manufacture was left in the hands of the established British and French companies. Furthermore, although there was some collaboration between the two countries, aircraft were built essentially to meet the requirements of their respective national airlines and consequently failed to make a real impact in the international arena. Only the Vickers Viscount and the Sud-Aviation Caravelle were sold in appreciable numbers, but these could not prevent the US domination of the world market.

Yet, in terms of aviation technology Europe could not only hold its own, but often led the world in radical thought. An example was the wide-ranging partnership between the French and British industries on the supersonic Concorde, which, while a tremendous technological achievement — and still the only supersonic aircraft in service — unfortunately swallowed up most of the available research and development money.

However, the public soon got the taste for flying and the emergence of powerful new jet engines led manufacturers on both sides of the Atlantic to develop high-capacity 'wide-body' concepts. In Europe, specifications and requirements were developed in the UK by the Lighthill Committee and by a working party set up by the major European airlines. These focused on an aircraft carrying between 200 and 250 seats, with a design range of around 800 nautical miles (1,500km). In the UK, Hawker Siddeley Aviation (HSA) was proposing the 160-seat plus HS.132 and the 204-seat HS.134 as high-capacity successors to the Trident, powered by two new-technology rear-mounted 133.5kN (30,000lb) thrust Rolls-Royce RB178s.

Across the Channel, Bréguet was working on the similarly-sized but double-deck, Br124, powered by four Rolls-Royce Speys mounted in pairs under the wing, with twin-engined alternatives, using either the RB178 or Pratt & Whitney's JT9D turbofans also considered. Nord Aviation had the N600 on the drawing board, which was a high-wing design, also with four Speys, but with an unusual horizontal double-bubble fuselage, and 12-abreast seating for 250 passengers. Sud-Aviation's Galion was a single-deck version for 200 passengers, six-abreast, with a double-deck alternative for up to 250 passengers. France's other aircraft manufacturer, Avions Marcel Dassault, evaluated a 220-seat double-deck design with the engines mounted under a low wing. All these designs were much closer in size to the A310, than to the A300 which reached production status first.

COLLABORATING ON AN IDEA

The word Airbus was already being coined by some, but the governments of the United Kingdom, France and Germany (which wanted to re-establish its industry,) realised the enormous financial and technical investment that would be required to produce several such aircraft independently. Instead they urged their manufacturers to enter into working partnerships, to produce a single acceptable design. The French and British governments jointly drew up a paper in 1964 entitled *An Outline Requirement for an Ultra High-Capacity Short-Range Aircraft*, which set out the guidelines for this new-generation airliner, conditional upon cross-Channel collaboration.

British Aircraft Corporation (BAC) and Sud-Aviation met in July 1964 to discuss a 180-200-seat short/medium-range aircraft, but serious dialogue between France and the United Kingdom at government level did not begin until June the following year, when France also initiated high-level talks with the German industry.

Prompted by the UK government's rejection of the HS.134, HSA entered into discussions with Bréguet and Nord Aviation, while BAC initiated talks with Sud-Aviation and Dassault about possible co-operation on the Galion. The more fanciful ideas were discarded along the way and what emerged from the Hawker/Bréguet/Nord team was the fairly conventional 200-250 seat HBN 100, which proposed a circular fuselage and two high by-pass ratio turbofan engines mounted under the low wing with a 30° sweep. Four back-up designs were discarded for various practical reasons, leaving the HBN 100 as the design that formed the basis of what was to become the Airbus.

Germany proved the most enthusiastic partner by setting up an Airbus Study Group in July, which brought together Dornier, Hamburger Flugzeugbau (HFB), Messerschmitt, Siebelwerke and Vereinigte Flugtechnische Werke (VFW), later formalised as Deutsche Airbus. The German, French and British manufacturers presented a joint concept document to

ABOVE: The first artist's impression of the proposed twin-engined, widebody Airbus.

the governments on 15 October 1966, which was approved at a trilateral ministerial meeting held in Paris on 9 May 1967. Four months later, a Memorandum of Understanding (MoU) authorised continued design studies and project definition and nominated Sud-Aviation, Hawker Siddeley and Deutsche Airbus, as the airframe partners.

After discarding earlier plans for total French leadership, with the others acting as subcontractors, it was agreed that Sud-Aviation would have design leadership for the airframe, in exchange for Rolls-Royce leadership on the engine. Britain and France were to contribute 37.5 percent to the first phase development costs, with Germany providing the balance. Britain was also to be responsible for 75 percent of the engine development costs, while France and Germany shared the remainder. Broad agreement was also reached on the distribution of work, which was roughly in proportion to the financial input of the partner nations.

In addition to design leadership, Sud-Aviation took responsibility for the flight deck, nose and fuselage centre section, engine installation, most of the systems definition and final assembly. Hawker Siddeley was given design and production responsibility for the wing, while Deutsche Airbus was charged with producing the remainder of the fuselage, the tailplane, and definition and design of the passenger cabin, cargo holds and installation of the auxiliary power unit (APU).

But it was far from plain sailing from then on. The French government nearly cancelled the Airbus project in favour of the Dassault Mercure, and the lack of agreement on the size of the aircraft, and the fact that neither Air France nor Lufthansa had placed orders, plunged the whole project into serious jeopardy in 1968. This was followed by Britain's surprise withdrawal on 10 April 1969. Rolls-Royce also found the new US tri-jets a much more lucrative market for its smaller RB.211 engine. France and Germany, however, forged ahead and a final devel-

opment contract was signed on 29 May 1969, which covered the prototype phase and extended for one year after certification of the basic type. The retention of Hawker Siddeley was essential to move the project forward, and it was to the company's great credit, that it decided to continue as a privileged subcontractor, partly using its own funds.

Airbus Industrie was set up on 18 December 1970 as a Groupement d'Intérets Economique (GIE) under French law, created specifically to facilitate the formation of co-operative ventures, for which existing legislation proved too restrictive. The GIE provides considerable operational flexibility and enables third parties to deal with a single entity. In the interim a number of changes had taken place, some of which affected the composition of the GIE. In France, Sud-Aviation and Nord Aviation had merged on 1 January 1970 to form Aerospatiale, while in Germany, Dornier withdrew from Deutsche Airbus to pursue an independent path. A subsequent rationalisation of Germany's manufacturing capabilities brought together HFB, Messerschmitt and Siebel under the MBB (Messerschmitt-Bölkow-Blohm) banner, with VFW linking up with Fokker in the Netherlands.

At the end of 1970 the Dutch government decided to join the programme but elected not to become a full member. One year later, Spain came into Airbus, taking a 4.2 percent stake in equal portions from the German and French participation. The share was based on the value of the horizontal tailplane, which was to be taken over from MBB by Spanish manufacturer CASA. Shareholding in Airbus Industrie was then distributed among Aerospatiale (47.9 percent), Deutsche Airbus (47.9 percent) and CASA (4.2 percent). It remained so until Britain rejoined the consortium on 1 January 1979, taking a 20 percent stake, with 10 percent each coming from Aerospatiale and Deutsche Airbus.

SMALLER IS BEAUTIFUL

Specific design requirements had been discussed at the first intergovernmental meeting between Germany, France and Great Britain as early as March 1966, and by the time the project definition phase had been agreed upon on 25 July 1967, the Airbus had grown in size to accommodate 267 passengers. It was then powered by two RB207 engines generating a static thrust of 211kN (47,500lb) each.

But with British European Airways (BEA) concerned that the Airbus was too large and would in any case would be too late to meet its own requirements for a complementary type to the 1-11, BAC firmed up its 2-11 design. The BAC 2-11 was based on carrying 208 passengers a distance of 1,300 nautical miles (2,400km), but had one significant drawback in that it was not a wide-body. BEA initially wanted 12 aircraft for its high-density business and tourist routes by summer 1972, but soon revised its estimate upward to between 30 and 40 aircraft. But the British government, wanting to be seen as pro-European, refused to fund development of the 2-11. The decision was a huge disappointment to BAC, as evidence gathered from European airlines pointed to a market for 1,500 aircraft of that size. Questions were being asked about the government's

logic of supporting a 300-seater, which only Air France and Air Inter seemed to find acceptable.

BEA was later to get the same response from the government regarding the 220-seat BAC 3-11, but for different reasons. A larger aircraft with a similar specification to the Airbus, the 3-11 represented direct competition to the European aircraft. It made little commercial sense to have two competing aircraft in Europe, but BAC appeared to be winning the argument in the corridors of power, until a change of government turned everything upside down. Aviation was low on the priority list of the new Conservative administration, which, on 3 November 1970, announced that it would not fund the 3-11, nor Britain's re-entry into Airbus, which until then had once again been under consideration. In the end, BEA got neither the 2-11 nor the 3-11, which were both to be powered by Rolls-Royce engines. Much to the chagrin of Airbus and supporters of the European industry, the British flag-carrier (which soon became known as British Airways) opted to throw in its lot with Boeing and did not place its first order for an Airbus until nearly 30 years later.

Airbus could not completely ignore the overwhelming evidence for a smaller aircraft, and details of a scaled-down version for 250 seats, designated at first the A250 and then the A300B, were released on 11 December 1968. The General Electric CF6-50 turbofan, which was being proposed for the DC-10, the Pratt & Whitney JT9D, and the Rolls-Royce RB.211 being developed for the Lockheed TriStar, were now all within the required power range. For some, it was still too large, and one of the main target customers, the German flag-carrier Lufthansa, remained convinced that even at 250 seats, the A300B would not be required for another 10 years.

But it soon became clear that the French airlines called the tune. Air France, anticipating an upswing in business traffic within Europe, began pressing for 24 more passengers in the Airbus. This was achieved by inserting two extra fuselage frames ahead and three aft of the wings, providing space for three more rows of eight seats and boosting capacity up to 281 passengers in an eight-abreast, two-aisle configuration, with seating for 345 nine-abreast passengers possible. An overall improvement in economics ensured that this model, known as the A300B2, was the first to enter airline service with Air France on 23 May 1974.

The French carrier had also become the first to order the A300B2 in November 1971, a year before the first flight on 28 October 1972. Lufthansa, however, had little enthusiasm for the aircraft and did not announce its intention to order the A300B2 until after the aircraft had flown, and then only for three aircraft. Its belated decision had more to do with pressure from the German government, which had invested heavily in the Airbus programme, than with its own desire to purchase an aircraft it still considered one size too big.

ABOVE LEFT: *Signing of the Franco-German agreement for the joint development of the Airbus at Le Bourget on 29 May.*

LEFT: *Henri Ziegler signs loan agreement with the European Investment Bank (EIB) in Luxembourg in December 1971.*

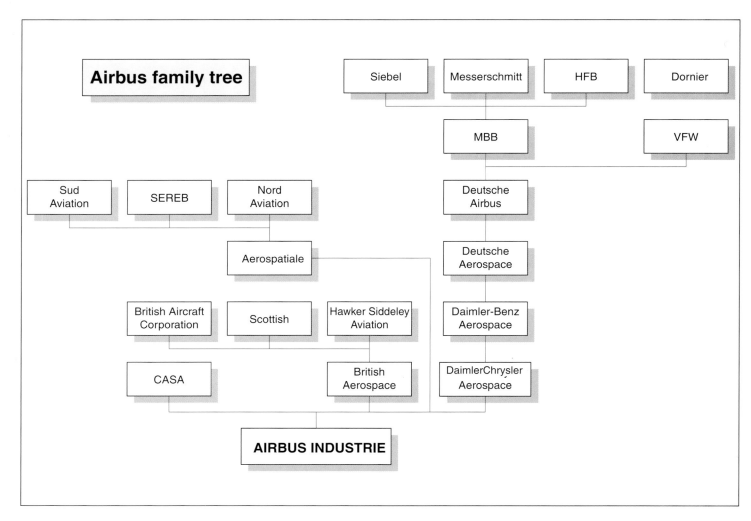

Airbus family tree

ABOVE: Airbus Industrie family tree.

ABOVE RIGHT: Airbus Industrie headquarters in Toulouse.

RIGHT: The multi-national nature of Airbus is demonstrated by the national flags surrounding its respected symbol.

But Lufthansa would not be denied, and when British Airways (formed out of British Overseas Airways Corporation [BOAC] and BEA on 1 April 1972) issued a requirement for a 200-seat RTOL (Reduced Take-Off and Landing) aircraft to be powered by Rolls-Royce RB.211 turbofans, Airbus began to take notice. A sluggish order book in the early years for the A300 may also have prompted Airbus to revisit the development of a smaller variant, although it had always enthusiastically embraced the concept of a family of aircraft. But, according to some, it had made a mistake in building the A300 before the A310. The British Airways requirement led to the A300B10 proposal, which offered a typical seating capacity of 210 passengers in a fuselage some 22.9ft (7m) shorter. Normal range was set at around 1,750 nautical miles (3,240km).

The manufacturer's initial approach was to maintain maximum commonality with the A300, and the changes originally envisaged were confined to a shortening of the A300B2 fuselage and a simplification of the high lift system. This so-called minimum-change B10MC was born out of a desire by Airbus to bring a new aircraft onto the market as quickly as possible and without too many risks. But several interesting years were to pass before the final specification was settled, having largely been shaped by two airlines and, equally crucially, by aviation developments on the other side of the Atlantic.

TRANS-ATLANTIC SHUTTLE
Over on the US West Coast, Airbus' main competitors Boeing and McDonnell Douglas became increasingly active in the short-haul sector. McDonnell Douglas had always had a DC-10 twin for short stage lengths on the drawing board, and with Europe forging ahead with the A300, the concept was pushed once more to the forefront to provide US competition. But McDonnell Douglas quickly realised that it could not meet the required economics over shorter ranges simply by scaling down the existing tri-jet. The AMRA (Advanced Medium-Range Aircraft) underwent several design changes before being promoted in September 1976 under the designation DC-X-200, being able to carry 198 passengers a distance of 2,700 nautical miles (5,000km). Although it incorporated a new supercritical wing and used advanced materials including composites, the cockpit showed only minor modification from that of the DC-10.

Boeing's 7X7 proposal, on the other hand, was a tri-jet with a T-tail configuration and essentially a double-deck

Boeing 727 in appearance, although considerably more advanced. New technology included an improved aerofoil to allow thicker, higher aspect ratio wings, improved aluminium alloys and a limited use of composites, and digital electronics in controls and instrumentation. It projected a typical passenger capacity of 200 in a mixed-class US domestic configuration, with a maximum eight-abreast seating possible, and US transcontinental range capability. Up to 16 LDR containers could be carried in the underfloor cargo deck. Development of the 7X7 was a joint activity between Boeing and Aeritalia (the latter had a 20 percent stake in the programme), with Japan as a likely future partner. In the end the project was abandoned, Boeing following Airbus' lead in twin-engined design with the 757, 767 and 777 products.

In parallel with these projects, neither of which came to fruition, both US manufacturers approached Airbus Industrie for the purpose of exploring possible collaboration on a joint US-European project. In a message delivered to Airbus in spring 1976, Boeing proposed an airliner with a new Boeing wing, and the much-admired Airbus fuselage — the cross-section chosen by Airbus provided a far better freight capability than the smaller fuselage diameter of Boeing aircraft. The offer was taken seriously and for some time, dialogue between the two manufacturers continued both in Seattle and Toulouse. The joint project was given the designation BB10.

Airbuses flying over the Alps.

However, the talks, while showing potential, also raised suspicions within Airbus about the precise long-term motives of the US manufacturers. The Americans, after all, had only a few years previously dismissed the European undertaking as a short-lived phenomenon — but they now found themselves being forced to take the threat to their traditional market domination seriously. In the end, Airbus concluded that the reasons behind the apparent wish for a partnership were coloured by a hidden agenda, designed to weaken the organisation at a time when it was moving into top gear.

The end result was that, due to entrenched national interests on both sides, no joint proposals emerged. The B10, therefore, proceeded as a solely European project and was greatly influenced by the requirements of Lufthansa and Swissair, as well as some of the major US trunk airlines, although of the latter only Pan American World Airways eventually bought the new type.

2 DESIGN AND PRODUCTION

The minimum change aircraft offered an easy solution, but Lufthansa, the most likely launch customer, could not be persuaded. The new technologies that were being considered in America also suggested that producing such a variant would represent a retrograde step. That Europe needed a short-haul, medium-capacity aircraft for the 1980s was outlined in a Lufthansa study document revealed in October 1975. In that document, Lufthansa accepted that with the existing capacity of Airbus Industrie and the financial support that can be expected, the A300B10 project was the best approach to the EURAC (European Aircraft) concept, which stood a chance of being realised.

However, it listed several drawbacks compared to the optimum design. Three of these were rather fundamental to its own requirement and included range, wings and fuselage. Lufthansa

said that the range far exceeded requirements resulting in unnecessarily high take-off and structural weight, that the wing was too large and too heavy for an optimum range of 2,000nm (3,704km), and that the slenderness of the rear fuselage made for poor utilisation. In their place, it proposed

- A new lighter transonic wing with a sweep of approximately 20°, aspect ratio of 9, and a profile thickness of some 13-14 percent

- A wing span of 141ft 1in (43m) and area of 2,260ft^2 (210m^2)

- Accommodation for 196 passengers at a 34in (860mm) seat pitch, in a circular fuselage from nose to tail

Apart from being a much more advanced and smaller aircraft, Lufthansa also considered that its proposal would eliminate the possible competition with the A300B2/B4, while retaining

A310 model in the wind tunnel at Hatfield.

LEFT: Computer-aided design used by British Aerospace Airbus at Chester.

RIGHT: Four Super Guppies transported Airbus assemblies between the various production plants until replaced by the Beluga from 1996.

The final specification was still to be issued, but the MoU stipulated that it had to be completed by 31 March 1979. Some two weeks before that date, Swissair signed a formal contract for 10 aircraft, plus 10 options, with Lufthansa signing on 2 April for a massive 25 firm and 25 options, which included the conversion of nine A300 options. Interestingly, West Africa's multi-national carrier Air Afrique had slipped in between the Swissair and Lufthansa orders, signing a contract for two aircraft on 31 March 1979. KLM Royal Dutch Airlines and Air France were not far behind, signing up for 10 and 5 aircraft, plus options on 3 April and 9 May respectively. Thus within eight weeks, the firm order book for the A310 had signatures for 52 aircraft.

commonality with the A300B2/B4 and partially with the DC-10-30 in engines and systems. The General Electric CF6-50C engines were to be retained, although operated at reduced thrust, but modifications were needed to the landing gear to take account of the reduced weight, and to the tail unit.

Over the months following the Lufthansa document, discussions with the Airbus partners intensified. The proposed new wing entered seriously into calculations for the first time in March 1976, although every avenue was explored in using a modified A300 wing to keep the costs down. While Airbus agreed with Lufthansa that the application of new advanced technology was essential in moving the project forward, it remained concerned (given the previous history of other European aircraft) about tailoring it too closely to the specifications demanded by a single airline.

However, work continued between Lufthansa and Swissair towards a detailed specification which would suit both carriers. Lufthansa needed an aircraft to fill the gap between the A300 and its Boeing 727s, while the Swiss carrier needed an economic aircraft sized between its McDonnell Douglas DC-10-30s and MD-81s. Thus their requirements were not dissimilar, and when other airlines began to support the project, the A300B10MC was abandoned at the end of 1976.

On 1 September 1977, Lufthansa and Swissair agreed to define a joint specification, which was completed on 9 June 1978. But the real breakthrough came the following month, when both carriers signed a memorandum of understanding (MoU) for a total of 16 A300-10s. The designation A300-10 was soon dropped in favour of A310, to indicate that it was a new aircraft, rather than merely a variant of the A300.

BRITAIN RETURNS TO THE FOLD

By 1978, Britain had let it be known that it would be interested in re-joining Airbus, although British Aerospace meanwhile had also been in advanced discussions with Boeing to become a risk-sharing partner in the 757 twinjet programme. The debate within the British establishment on the respective merits of either becoming a full member of the Airbus consortium and influence aircraft development in Europe, or instead becoming a sub-contractor to US manufacturers, was lengthy and often heated. But it was not only up to Britain. While Airbus Industrie realised the benefits of having another risk-sharing partner willing to provide the financial support necessary to launch a new aircraft, the French government had not forgotten nor forgiven Britain for pulling out in 1969, at a critical time in the development of the Airbus.

France demanded that an order from at least one British airline was the minimum commitment that should be expected in return for admitting the country back into Airbus. An offer was made to include the Rolls-Royce RB.211 as an alternative power plant, to make the A310 more attractive to British Airways. Much to the consternation of the French in particular, the flag-carrier snubbed the A310 and in September 1978 ordered the Boeing 757 instead. The timing of the announcement was distinctly unfortunate, as just days earlier, the Airbus Industrie partners and British Aerospace had initialled an agreement for BAe's entry as a full partner. The following negotiations were protracted and delicate, to say the least, but

on 29 November 1978, BAe's full partnership agreement received the official signature and the British company took a 20 percent stake in Airbus Industrie with effect from 1 January 1979.

It was now imperative that detailed work on the A310 proceeded without delay, if Airbus was not to fall behind Boeing — which had reached an advanced stage in the development of the 757 and 767 models, with the latter especially considered a close competitor. Work on a new wing had been in progress at VFW-Fokker in Germany and at BAe Hatfield. But following the re-admission of Britain, and against strong objections from Aerospatiale, responsibility for the overall design and manufacture was given to British Aerospace, with VFW-Fokker responsible for the moving surfaces. After testing several configurations in the wind tunnel, the designers decided to maintain the 28° sweepback and virtually the same span as the A300. It was found, however, that through the use of a new aerofoil section with a double curvature in the lower skin of the inner section, the wing area could be reduced by 16 percent. The increased strength also helped to produce weight savings of more than 5 tonnes.

Leading edge slats of greater chord and radius were introduced to improve take-off performance, while cruise drag was reduced by combining the two outer flaps into one, with the inner flaps changed from the original tabbed-Fowler flaps on the A300 to a vaned Fowler flap. It was also found that the outboard ailerons could be removed, producing a much cleaner wing. The pylons were designed to support all advanced technology, high bypass turbofan engines with a thrust of around 213kN (48,000lb), then available for the A310. These included the General Electric CF6-80A1 and Pratt & Whitney JT9D-7R4D1, although Airbus was prepared to fit the Rolls-Royce RB211-524D4, if requested. However, as no orders had been received by the time the first flight approached, the certification programme was carried out only with the US engines, and these remained the only ones to power the A310.

The fuselage was reshaped at the rear and cut shorter by the removal of 13 frames from that of the A300, while the fin required few modifications, except for a reduced size horizontal stabiliser. But the most striking innovation in the A310 was the application of the latest advances in avionics technology, so that the aircraft could be operated by two pilots, rather than the two pilots and flight engineer prevalent in other aircraft on both sides of the Atlantic.

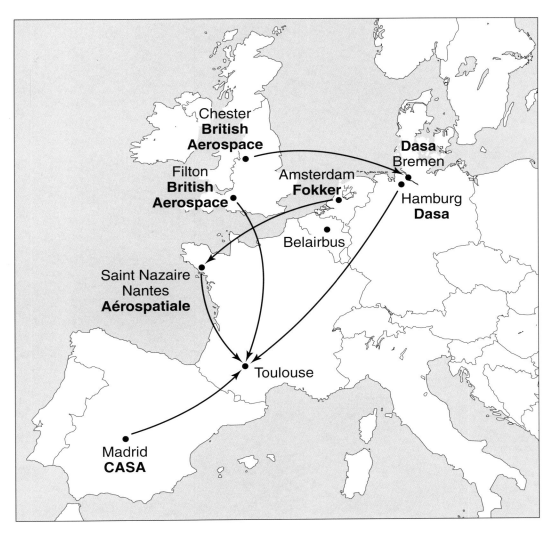

ABOVE: Production flow.

In what Airbus called the FFCC (Forward Facing Crew Cockpit), the sideways facing flight engineer's panel was removed and all instruments and controls were arranged in front of, or within easy reach, above the crew. Six full-colour CRT (Cathode Ray Tube) electronic displays for the EFIS (Electronic Flight Information System) and ECAM (Electronic Centralised Aircraft Monitor) replaced the analogue electro-mechanical dials. Airbus also brought in German luxury car-maker Porsche to create a comfortable working environment to complement the new technology. The result was increased efficiency on the flight deck and a reduced mental and physical workload for the crew, which in turn has the added benefit of enhanced safety.

To arrive at the final aerodynamic configuration of the aircraft, many models of the A310 at varying scales, including 1:38 with a wing span of 3ft 11in (1.20m), were 'flown' in wind tunnels at Emmen (Switzerland), Göttingen (Germany), at the NRL in the Netherlands, RAE Farnborough (UK) and at Modane in France.

WORK SHARE AND PRODUCTION
The sharing of design work and production followed a similar pattern to that established for A300, although there are some differences in organisation and some elements of work share. It is still, however, shared among the partners roughly in proportion to their financial holdings in the consortium. Aerospatiale builds the nose section (including the flightdeck), lower centre fuselage and wing box, rear wing-body fairings, engine pylons and airbrakes, and is also responsible for final assembly. DaimlerChrysler Aerospace Airbus, formerly Deutsche Aerospace Airbus and Daimler-Benz Aerospace Airbus, is responsible for the forward fuselage and associated doors, tailcone, fin and rudder, and flaps and spoilers. It also fits control surfaces and equipment to the main wing structure produced by British Aerospace. CASA's contribution includes horizontal tail surfaces, nose gear and mainwheel doors, and forward passenger doors, while Fokker manufactures the main undercarriage leg and hinged fairing doors, wingtips and fence, all-speed ailerons and flap track fairings. Belgium's Belairbus (which became a subcontractor on the A310 on 6 April 1979) produces the wing leading-edge slats and forward wing/fuselage fairings. After the bankruptcy of Fokker Aircraft on 15 March 1996, the responsibility for production and support of the A310 was transferred to Fokker Aviation, which became part of the Dutch engineering group Stork on 18 July 1996.

PROJECTED TWIN-ENGINED AIRBUS VERSIONS

	B1	B2	B3	B4
Wing span	44.83m	44.83m	44.83m	44.83m
	147ft 1in	147ft 1in	147ft 1in	147ft 1in
Length	50.95m	53.60m	50.95m	53.60m
	167ft 2in	175ft 10in	167ft 2in	175ft 10in
Accommodation (typ)	257	281	257	281
Power Plant	CF6-50A	CF6-50C	CF6-50C	CF6-50C
MTOW	132,000kg	137,000kg	148,500kg	150,000kg
	291,000lb	302,030lb	327,400lb	330,690lb
MLW	120,000kg	127,500kg	131,000kg	133,000kg
	264,550lb	281,090lb	288,800lb	293,210lb
MZFW	109,000kg	116,500kg	122,000kg	122,000kg
	240,300lb	256,840lb	268,960lb	268,960lb
Typical range	1,150nm	1,750nm	1,750nm	2,100nm
	2,130km	3,240km	3,240km	3,885km

	B5	B6	B7	B8
Wing span	44.83m	44.83m	44.83m	45.75m
	147ft 1in	147ft 1in	147ft 1in	150ft 1in
Length	50.95m	53.60m	54.65m	50.95m
	167ft 2in	175ft 10in	179ft 4in	167ft 2in
Accommodation type	cargo	cargo	290	257
Power Plant	CF6-50A	CF6-50C	RB	CF6-6
MTOW	132,000kg	150,000kg	148,500kg	124,000kg
	291,000lb	330,690lb	327,400lb	273,370lb
MLW	120,000kg	133,000kg	131,000kg	114,000kg
	264,550lb	293,210lb	288,800lb	351,325lb
MZFW	109,000kg	116,500kg	120,000kg	105,000kg
	240,300lb	256,840lb	264,550lb	231,480lb
Typical range	1,150nm	2,100nm	1,600nm	1,000nm
	2,130km	3,885km	2,960km	1,850km

	B9*	B10**	
Wing span	44.83m	43.90m	
	147ft 1in	144ft	* later developed into the A330
Length	57.27m	46.66m	** became the A310
	187ft 11in	153ft 1in	
Accommodation type	309	210	MTOW Max take-off weight
Power Plant	CF6-50C	CF6-50C	MLW Max landing weight
MTOW	150,000kg	121,000kg	MZFW Max zero-fuel weight
	330,690lb	266,755lb	
MLW	135,000kg	115,000kg	
	297,620lb	253,530lb	
MZFW	125,000kg	95,000kg	
	275,575lb	209,450lb	
Typical range	2,160nm	1,750nm	
	4,000km	3,2,40km	

As on the A300, this approach clearly necessitated a wide geographical spread of manufacture, but had already been proven over the 10 years since the A300 began life on the production life. While still greater distances were overcome in the United States, there was (and is) a fundamental difference in the Airbus approach, which sets it apart.

Right from its inception, Airbus had planned that all partners would contribute complete subassemblies in a 'ready-to-fly' condition, with all cables, pipe runs and equipment installed and checked, rather than merely becoming a manufacturer of parts and components. The result was that just 4 percent of man-hours required in building the Airbus models are spent on the final assembly line in Toulouse, which equates to around one-fifth of the work required by traditional methods.

The large and heavy subassemblies basically ruled out transport by road on a long-term basis, while sections were also too large for moving by rail. The obvious alternative, sea transport, was considered much too slow. As a result, and following

ABOVE: A310 wing out of the jig at Chester.

LEFT: A busy A310 assembly line at Toulouse.

BELOW: A310 being wheeled into the hangar for final completion.

OVER PAGE: The A300-600ST Super Transporter 'Beluga' now transports all Airbus parts to Toulouse for final assembly.

A310 production sharing

- Aérospatiale
- DaimlerChrysler Aerospace Airbus
- British Aerospace Airbus
- CASA
- Belairbus
- Fokker
- GE, PW
- Messier

on from the successful A300 operation, A310 sub-assemblies were flown by the two Aero Spacelines Guppy outsize freighters. As Airbus orders and production rates increased, UTA Industries at Le Bourget in Paris acquired the production rights and built two more Guppy 201s, which entered service in 1982 and 1983. All four were flown by UTA subsidiary Aéromaritime until 1989, when Airbus Industrie took direct control of the operation.

Known as Airbus Skylink 1, 2, 3 and 4, the four aircraft provided round-the-clock service, transporting wing, fuselage and tail assemblies from the various manufacturing sites of the Airbus partners in France, Germany, Spain and the UK. Each complete A310 required a total of eight flights, which amounted to some 45 hours in the air and a distance flown of 7,000nm (nearly 13,000km). With its swing-out nose section opening through 110°, a 25ft 6in (7.77m) diameter cargo hold and a maximum payload of 22 tonnes (???), the Guppy 201 could easily accommodate the largest and heaviest A310 sections.

With production rates increasing and new larger models added to the Airbus family, a bigger and faster aircraft was required, and from January 1996, the transportation of assemblies for all Airbus models, including the A310, was taken over by the new A300B4-600ST Super Transporter, named appropriately the Beluga. The aircraft shares an impressive commonality with the A300-600R, yet bears little physical resemblance

ABOVE: Production Sharing.

ABOVE RIGHT: Test equipment and ballast in the prototype.

BELOW RIGHT: The new two-crew digital cockpit.

and is virtually a new aircraft, although some 80 percent of the airframe structure is identical, and includes the wings, General Electric CF6-80C2A8 turbofan engines, landing gear, most of the lower fuselage, and the pressurised flightdeck. The most notable structural changes are a new cavernous upper fuselage joined to the lower section at the normal wing/fuselage line, and a re-positioned flightdeck below the main deck floor. This arrangement permits straight in loading through the largest single-piece, upward-opening freight door ever to be fitted to an aircraft.

In comparison with the Guppy, the Beluga carries 50 percent more volumetric load and is capable of transporting the largest single Airbus item. It has a payload of 47 tonnes more than double that of the Guppy, sufficient to carry heaviest section. The turbofan-powered aircraft is also considerably faster, and it is this speed advantage, together with a halving of the loading cycle through the use of special equipment installed at the manufacturing sites at Hamburg, Bremen, Chester and St Nazaire, that has enabled a reduction in the transport time of a

A310 FLIGHT TEST AIRCRAFT

AIRCRAFT	C/N	REGISTRATION	ENGINE	FIRST FLIGHT	
1	0162	F-WZLH	JT9D-7R4D1	03/04/1982	
2	0172	F-WZLI	JT9D-7R4D1	13/05/1982	
3	0191	F-WZLJ	CF6-80A	05/08/1982	TOTAL FLIGHT
4	0201	F-WZLK	CF6-80A	20/10/1982	TEST HOURS
5	0217	F-WZLL	JT9D-7R4D1	01/12/1982	**1,680**

complete Airbus from 45 hours to 19 hours.

The last of the four Guppies left Toulouse on 22 October 1997 on delivery to the National Aeronautics and Space Administration (NASA) at Houston, Texas, where it remains in regular use. The other three have been preserved at Toulouse, Bruntingthorpe, UK, and at Hamburg in Germany.

LIFT-OFF

After the completion of final assembly, the A310 was rolled out of the hangar at Toulouse on 16 February 1982 to make its public debut. It was painted in full Swissair colours on the right hand side and in Lufthansa's livery on the left, in recognition of the vital part played by the two launch customers in the development of the aircraft.

At 08:33 on the morning of 3 April 1982, the A310 (F-WZLH) lifted off the runway at Toulouse on its maiden flight, the first time a widebody jet had taken off with a two-crew cockpit. The flight crew consisted of chief test pilot Bernard Ziegler, co-pilot Pierre Baud, and flight test engineers Gérard Guyot, Günter Scherer and Jean-Pierre Flamant.

Bernard Ziegler took the new Airbus through a multitude of manoeuvres during the three hour 15 minutes test flight, many of which exceeded those normally carried out on such an occasion and demonstrated the integrity of the design at an early stage. The A310 climbed to an impressive 30,840ft (9,400m), and reached a speed of more than 300 knots (Mach 0.77), before dazzling onlookers with a slow flypast. Slats were extended for 30° banked turns, mixed with flight phases in a clean configuration, with slats and flaps fully retracted. The exploration of a wide range of yaw and roll movements were

LEFT: A striking head-on view of the A310.

BELOW: The first A310 F-WZLH, painted in the colours of launch customer Lufthansa on the port side, takes off on its maiden flight on 3 April 1982.

also part of the programme. Throughout the flight, the Pratt & Whitney JT9D-7R4D1 turbofan engines behaved impeccably. After touching down, Bernard Ziegler said:

'We achieved all our targets for the first flight. It was a completely problem-free flight, which didn't surprise us. This new bird flies just as pleasantly as its older brother, the A300.'

Pierre Baud added that during the flight 'all systems worked without problems and completely fulfiled their task of minimising crew workload and (achieving) a more economic conduct of the flight. We can say that this is the result of our extensive work in the simulator.' This point was backed up by Ziegler who observed that the crew 'felt at home' in the new environment the minute they climbed aboard. All were agreed that the aircraft had opened the door to a new future.

Five aircraft were assigned to the test and certification programme, three of which undertook the bulk of the work. In addition to Aircraft No.1, which carried out the first flight, the early workload was shared with Aircraft No.2 (F-WZLI), first flown on 13 May 1982 — at which time No.1 had already completed 210 hours of flying, 55 more than planned. Both were equipped with the JT9D-7R4D1, but were joined from 5 August 1982 by Aircraft No.3 (F-WZLJ), which was the first to be flown with the General Electric CF6-80A engines ordered by Lufthansa, and later tested a fly-by-wire system with side stick control. The remaining two, F-WZLK with

RIGHT: Aircraft No.1 was painted in launch customer Swissair colours on the right hand side.

BELOW: Fuel being jettisoned during a test flight.

General Electric engines and F-WZLL with Pratt & Whitney engines, flew on 20 October and 1 December 1982 respectively.

Aircraft No.1 was fitted with a small mini-wing attached to one wing tip, to test the wing's flutter characteristics. The 3ft 3in (1m) long mini-wing was mounted on a shaft and could be turned by a hydraulic motor to change the angle of attack, according to programmed frequencies and amplitudes. The oscillations resulting from the load changes could thus be studied throughout the total frequency spectrum, and proved that the wing itself could dampen even the strongest oscillations.

The lower rear fuselage section was also reinforced in the first aircraft for the rolling test, to prevent any damage while the nose was pulled up at a sharp angle during determination of the minimum take-off speed. Another interesting innovation was the replacement of the leading edges from the elevators by other less aerodynamic components, which were designed to simulate the build up of ice and back up the extensive wind tunnel tests during which the model was 'flown' surrounded by freezing liquids. Again, the actual flight tests demonstrated that even with heavy icing, degradation of aircraft behaviour and flight performance was minimal.

Airbus Industrie found very early in its test programme that the A310 exceeded almost all the predicted performance figures guaranteed to airline customers. For any given weight, the A310 was able to cruise 2,000ft (610m) higher than expected, while the economical cruising speed proved to be Mach 0.81, compared to the Mach 0.79 originally calculated. Another 4 percent improvement in fuel consumption over long range sectors could be offered, over and above an already economical operational envelope. As a result, handling trials could be completed early, with no changes necessary, which was unusual for a new type. The remaining months were spent largely on the development of electronics and software for the onboard computers, and it came as no surprise to Airbus that the uneventful test programme was completed ahead of schedule. The French and German authorities simultaneously issued the type certificate to the A310 on 11 March 1983, three weeks earlier than planned. The certificate covered both engine types, Category II approaches and two-crew operation. UK CAA certification was obtained in January 1984 and US Federal Aviation Administration (FAA) certification early in 1985. The European Joint Aviation Authorities (JAA) granted Category IIIa approval in September 1983, and Category IIIb in November the following year.

The A310 had accumulated a total of 1,680 hours in 692 flights, operated from 33 airports and was flown by more than 80 crews from Airbus Industrie, the French and German certification authorities and customer airlines. On 29 March, two weeks after the original certification, Swissair and Lufthansa formerly took delivery of their first aircraft in a ceremony in Toulouse. On the same day, the Swiss flag-carrier also announced that it would change four of its order for the A310-200 to the new extended range A310-300 variant, then under development. The firm order book by that time had surpassed the 100 mark.

3 Technical Specification

	A310-200	A310-200	A310-200	A310-200	A310-200C
External dimensions					
Wingspan	43.90m	43.90m	43.90m	43.90m	43.90m
	144ft 0¼in	144ft 0¼in	144ft 0¼in	144ft 0¼in	144ft 0¼in
Length overall	46.67m	46.67m	46.67m	46.67m	46.67m
	153ft 1½in	153ft 1½in	153ft 1½in	153ft 1½in	153ft 1½in
Height overall	15.81m	15.81m	15.81m	15.81m	15.81m
	51ft 10½in	51ft 10½in	51ft 10½in	51ft 10½in	51ft 10½in
Tailplane span	16.26m	16.26m	16.26m	16.26m	16.26m
	53ft 4¼in	53ft 4¼in	53ft 4¼in	53ft 4¼in	53ft 4¼in
Max fuselage diameter	5.64m	5.64m	5.64m	5.64m	5.64m
	18ft 6in	18ft 6in	18ft 6in	18ft 6in	18ft 6in
Wheel track	9.60m	9.60m	9.60m	9.60m	9.60m
	31ft 6in	31ft 6in	31ft 6in	31ft 6in	31ft 6in
Wheelbase	15.21m	15.21m	15.21m	15.21m	15.21m
	49ft 10¾in	49ft 10¾in	49ft 10¾in	49ft 10¾in	49ft 10¾in
Internal dimensions					
Main cabin length	33.25m	33.25m	33.25m	33.25m	33.25m
	109ft 1in	109ft 1in	109ft 1in	109ft 1in	109ft 1in
Max cabin width	5.28m	5.28m	5.28m	5.28m	5.28m
	17ft 4in	17ft 4in	117ft 4in	17ft 4in	17ft 4in
Max cabin height	2.33m	2.33m	2.33m	2.33m	2.33m
	7ft 7¾in	7ft 7¾in	7ft 7¾in	7ft 7¾in	7ft 7¾in
Areas					
Wing, gross m^2	$219m^2$	$219m^2$	$219m^2$	$219m^2$	$219m^2$
	2,358sq ft	2,358sq ft	2,358sq ft	2,358sq ft	2,358sq ft
Leading-edge slats	$28.54m^2$	$28.54m^2$	$28.54m^2$	$28.54m^2$	$28.54m^2$
	307.2sq ft	307.2sq ft	307.2sq ft	307.2sq ft	307.2sq ft
Krüger flaps	$1.12m^2$	$1.12m^2$	$1.12m^2$	$1.12m^2$	$1.12m^2$
	12sq ft	12sq ft	12sq ft	12sq ft	12sq ft
Trailing-edge flaps	$38.68m^2$	$38.68m^2$	$38.68m^2$	$38.68m^2$	$38.68m^2$
	516.4sq ft	516.4sq ft	516.4sq ft	516.4sq ft	516.4sq ft
Ailerons	$6.86m^2$	$6.86m^2$	$6.86m^2$	$6.86m^2$	$6.86m^2$
	73.84sq ft	73.84sq ft	73.84sq ft	73.84sq ft	73.84sq ft
Spoilers	$7.36m^2$	$7.36m^2$	$7.36m^2$	$7.36m^2$	$7.36m^2$
	79.22sq ft	79.22sq ft	79.22sq ft	79.22sq ft	79.22sq ft
Airbrakes	$6.16m^2$	$6.16m^2$	$6.16m^2$	$6.16m^2$	$6.16m^2$
	66.31sq ft	66.31sq ft	66.31sq ft	66.31sq ft	66.31sq ft
Fin	$45.24m^2$	$45.24m^2$	$45.24m^2$	$45.24m^2$	$45.24m^2$
	486.9sq ft	486.9sq ft	486.9sq ft	486.9sq ft	486.9sq ft
Rudder	$13.57m^2$	$13.57m^2$	$13.57m^2$	$13.57m^2$	$13.57m^2$
	146.1sq ft	146.1sq ft	146.1sq ft	146.1sq ft	146.1sq ft
Tailplane	$64m^2$	$64m^2$	$64m^2$	$64m^2$	$64m^2$
	689sq ft	689sq ft	689sq ft	689sq ft	689sq ft
Elevators	$19.20m^2$	$19.20m^2$	$19.20m^2$	$19.20m^2$	$19.20m^2$
	206.7sq ft	206.7sq ft	206.7sq ft	206.7sq ft	206.7sq ft

LEFT: The A310 fin comprises a main box, a removable leading edge, tear shrouds, a tip, and a single rudder, made almost entirely from composites.

BELOW: Carbon fibre fin box.

Carbon fibre fin box

- 95% reduction in components parts, excluding fasteners

- 22% weight saving (115kg / 256lb)

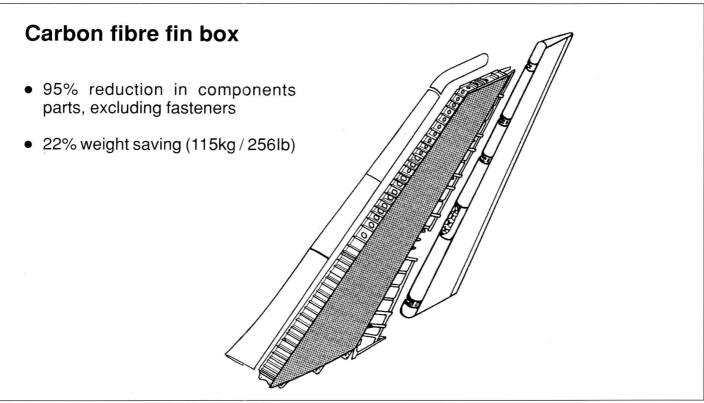

	A310-200	A310-200	A310-200	A310-200	A310-200C
Accommodation					
Passengers (typ/max)	220/280	220/280	220/280	220/280	220/280
Cargo volume	102.1cu m	102.1cu m	102.1cu m	102.1cu m	140cu m
	3,605cu.ft	3,605cu.ft	3,605cu.ft	3,605cu.ft	4,945cu.ft
Power plant					
Number and type	2 x CF6-80C2A2	2 x CF6-80A3	2 x JT9D-7R4D1	2 x PW4152	2 x CF6-80A3
Thrust (each)	238.1kN	222.4kN	213.5kN	231.4kN	222.4kN
	53,500lb	50,000lb	48,000lb	52,000lb	50,000lb
Weights and loadings					
Max take-off weight	142,000kg	142,000kg	142,000kg	142,000kg	142,000kg
	313,050lb	313,050lb	313,050lb	313,050lb	313,050lb
Max landing weight	123,000kg	123,000kg	123,000kg	123,000kg	123,000kg
	271,165lb	271,165lb	271,165lb	271,165lb	271,165lb
Max zero-fuel weight	113,000kg	113,000kg	113,000kg	113,000kg	113,000kg
	249,120lb	249,120lb	249,120lb	249,120lb	249,120lb
Operating wt empty	80,140kg	78,450kg	78,400kg	80,125kg	78,670kg
	176,685lb	172,950lb	172,840lb	176,645lb	173,435lb
Max payload	32,860kg	32,390kg	32,070kg	32,875kg	34,600kg
	72,445lb	71,405lb	70,700lb	72,475lb	76,280lb
Fuel capacity	54,920kg	54,920kg	54,920kg	54,920kg	54,920kg
	121,077lb	121,077lb	121,077lb	121,077lb	121,077lb

A310 general arrangement.

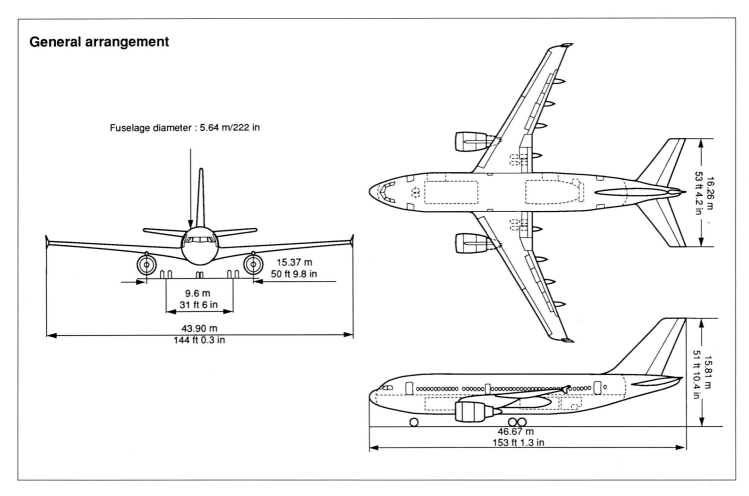

General arrangement

Fuselage diameter : 5.64 m/222 in

15.37 m
50 ft 9.8 in

9.6 m
31 ft 6 in

43.90 m
144 ft 0.3 in

16.26 m
53 ft 4.2 in

15.81 m
51 ft 10.4 in

46.67 m
153 ft 1.3 in

	A310-200	A310-200	A310-200	A310-200	A310-200C
Performance					
Max permitted operating speed (Vmo)					
	340kts	340kts	340kts	340kts	340kts
	629km/h	629km/h	629km/h	629km/h	629km/h
	391mph	391mph	391mph	391mph	391mph
Max operating speed (Mmo)	Mach 0.84	Mach 0.84	Mach 0.84	Mach 0.84	Mach 0.84
Typical cruise speed	457kts	457kts	457kts	457kts	457kts
	845km/h	845km/h	845km/h	845km/h	845km/h
	525mph	525mph	525mph	525mph	525mph
Approach speed (kts)	135kts	135kts	135kts	135kts	135kts
	250km/h	250km/h	250km/h	250km/h	250km/h
mph	155mph	155mph	155mph	155mph	155mph
Max operating altitude	12,500m	12,500m	12,500m	12,500m	12,500m
	41,000ft	41,000ft	41,000ft	41,000ft	41,000ft
Take-off field length	1,960m	1,951m	1,951m	1,890m	1,753m
	6,430ft	6,400ft	6,400ft	6,200ft	5,750ft
Landing field length	1,480m	1,630m	1,630m	1,555m	1,463m
	4,850ft	5,350ft	5,350ft	5,100ft	4,800ft
Range with typical payload	3,750nm	2,800nm	3,500nm	3,650nm	1,850nm
	6,940km	5,180km	6,475km	6,755km	3,425km
	4,310miles	3,220miles	4,020miles	4,200miles	2,125miles

	A310-300	A310-300	A310-300	A310-300	A310-300
External dimensions					
Wingspan	43.90m	43.90m	43.90m	43.90m	43.90m
	144ft 0¼in	144ft 0¼in	144ft 0¼in	144ft 0¼in	144ft 0¼in
Length overall	46.67m	46.67m	46.67m	46.67m	46.67m
	153ft 1½in	153ft 1½in	153ft 1½in	153ft 1½in	153ft 1½in
Height overall	15.81m	15.81m	15.81m	15.81m	15.81m
	51 ft 10½in	51 ft 10½in	51 ft 10½in	51 ft 10½in	51 ft 10½in
Tailplane span	16.26m	16.26m	16.26m	16.26m	16.26m
	53ft 4¼in	53ft 4¼in	53ft 4¼in	53ft 4¼in	53ft 4¼in
Max fuselage diameter	5.64m	5.64m	5.64m	5.64m	5.64m
	18 ft 6in	18 ft 6in	18 ft 6in	18 ft 6in	18 ft 6in
Wheel track	9.60m	9.60m	9.60m	9.60m	9.60m
	31ft 6in	31ft 6in	31ft 6in	31ft 6in	31ft 6in
Wheelbase	15.21m	15.21m	15.21m	15.21m	15.21m
	49ft 10¾in	49ft 10¾in	49ft 10¾in	49ft 10¾in	49ft 10¾in
Internal dimensions					
Main cabin length	33.25m	33.25m	33.25m	33.25m	33.25m
	109ft 1in	109ft 1in	109ft 1in	109ft 1in	109ft 1in
Max cabin width	5.28m	5.28m	5.28m	5.28m	5.28m
	17ft 4in	17ft 4in	17ft 4in	17ft 4in	17ft 4in
Max cabin height	2.33m	2.33m	2.33m	2.33m	2.33m
	7ft 7¾in	7ft 7¾in	7ft 7¾in	7ft 7¾in	7ft 7¾in
Areas					
Wing, gross	219m²	219m²	219m²	219m²	219m²
	2,358sq ft	2,358sq ft	2,358sq ft	2,358sq ft	2,358sq ft
Leading-edge slats	28.54m²	28.54m²	28.54m²	28.54m²	28.54m²
	307.2sq ft	307.2sq ft	307.2sq ft	307.2sq ft	307.2sq ft
Krüger flaps	1.12m²	1.12m²	1.12m²	1.12m²	1.12m²
	12sq ft	12sq ft	12sq ft	12sq ft	12sq ft
Trailing-edge flaps	38.68m²	38.68m²	38.68m²	38.68m²	38.68m²

	A310-300	A310-300	A310-300	A310-300	A310-300
	516.4sq ft	516.4sq ft	516.4sq ft	516.4sq ft	516.4sq ft
Ailerons	6.86m²	6.86m²	6.86m²	6.86m²	6.86m²
	73.84sq ft	73.84sq ft	73.84sq ft	73.84sq ft	73.84sq ft
Spoilers	7.36m²	7.36m²	7.36m²	7.36m²	7.36m²
	79.22sq ft	79.22sq ft	79.22sq ft	79.22sq ft	79.22sq ft
Airbrakes	6.16m²	6.16m²	6.16m²	6.16m²	6.16m²
	66.31sq ft	66.31sq ft	66.31sq ft	66.31sq ft	66.31sq ft
Fin	45.24m²	45.24m²	45.24m²	45.24m²	45.24m²
	486.9sq ft	486.9sq ft	486.9sq ft	486.9sq ft	486.9sq ft
Rudder	13.57m²	13.57m²	13.57m²	13.57m²	13.57m²
	146.1sq ft	146.1sq ft	146.1sq ft	146.1sq ft	146.1sq ft
Tailplane	64m²	64m²	64m²	64m²	64m²
	689sq ft	689sq ft	689sq ft	689sq ft	689sq ft
Elevators	19.20m²	19.20m²	19.20m²	19.20m²	19.20m²
	206.7sq ft	206.7sq ft	206.7sq ft	206.7sq ft	206.7sq ft

Accommodation

Passengers (typ/max)	220/280	220/280	220/280	220/280	220/280
Cargo volume	102.1cu m	102.1cu m	102.1cu m	102.1cu m	102.1cu m
cu.ft	3,605cu.ft	3,605cu.ft	3,605cu.ft	3,605cu.ft	3,605cu.ft

Power plant

Number and type	2 x CF6-80C2A2	2 x CF6-80C2A2	2 x CF6-80C2A8	2 x PW4152	2 x PW4152
Thrust (each)	238.1kN	238.1kN	262.5kN	231.4kN	231.4kN
	53,500lb	53,500lb	59,000lb	52,000lb	52,000lb

Weights and loadings

Max take-off weight	150,000kg	153,000kg	164,000kg	153,000kg	157,000kg
	330,690lb	337,305lb	361,555lb	337,305lb	346,120lb
Max landing weight	123,000kg	123,000kg	124,000kg	124,000kg	124,000kg
	271,165lb	271,165lb	273,370lb	273,370lb	271,165lb
Max zero-fuel weight	113,000kg	113,000kg	114,000kg	114,000kg	114,000kg
	249,120lb	249,120lb	251,325lb	251,325lb	251,325lb
Operating weight empty	81,205kg	81,205kg	81,610kg	81,165kg	81,165kg
	179,025lb	179,025lb	179,920lb	178,940lb	178,940lb
Max payload	28,970kg	34,590kg	32,390kg	34,600kg	34,600kg
	63,870lb	76,260lb	71,405lb	76,280lb	76,280lb
Fuel capacity	61,070kg	61,070kg	61,070kg	61,070kg	61,070kg
	134,635lb	134,635lb	134,635lb	134,635lb	134,635lb

Performance

Max permitted operating speed (Vmo)					
	360kts	340kts	340kts	340kts	340kts
	666km/h	629km/h	629km/h	629km/h	629km/h
mph	414mph	391mph	391mph	391mph	391mph
Max operating speed (Mmo)	Mach 0.84	Mach 0.84	Mach 0.84	Mach 0.84	Mach 0.84
Typical cruise speed	457kts	457kts	459kts	457kts	457kts
	845km/h	845km/h	849km/h	845km/h	845km/h
	525mph	525mph	527mph	525mph	525mph
Approach speed	135kts	135kts	135kts	135kts	135kts
	250km/h	250km/h	250km/h	250km/h	250km/h
	155mph	155mph	155mph	155mph	155mph

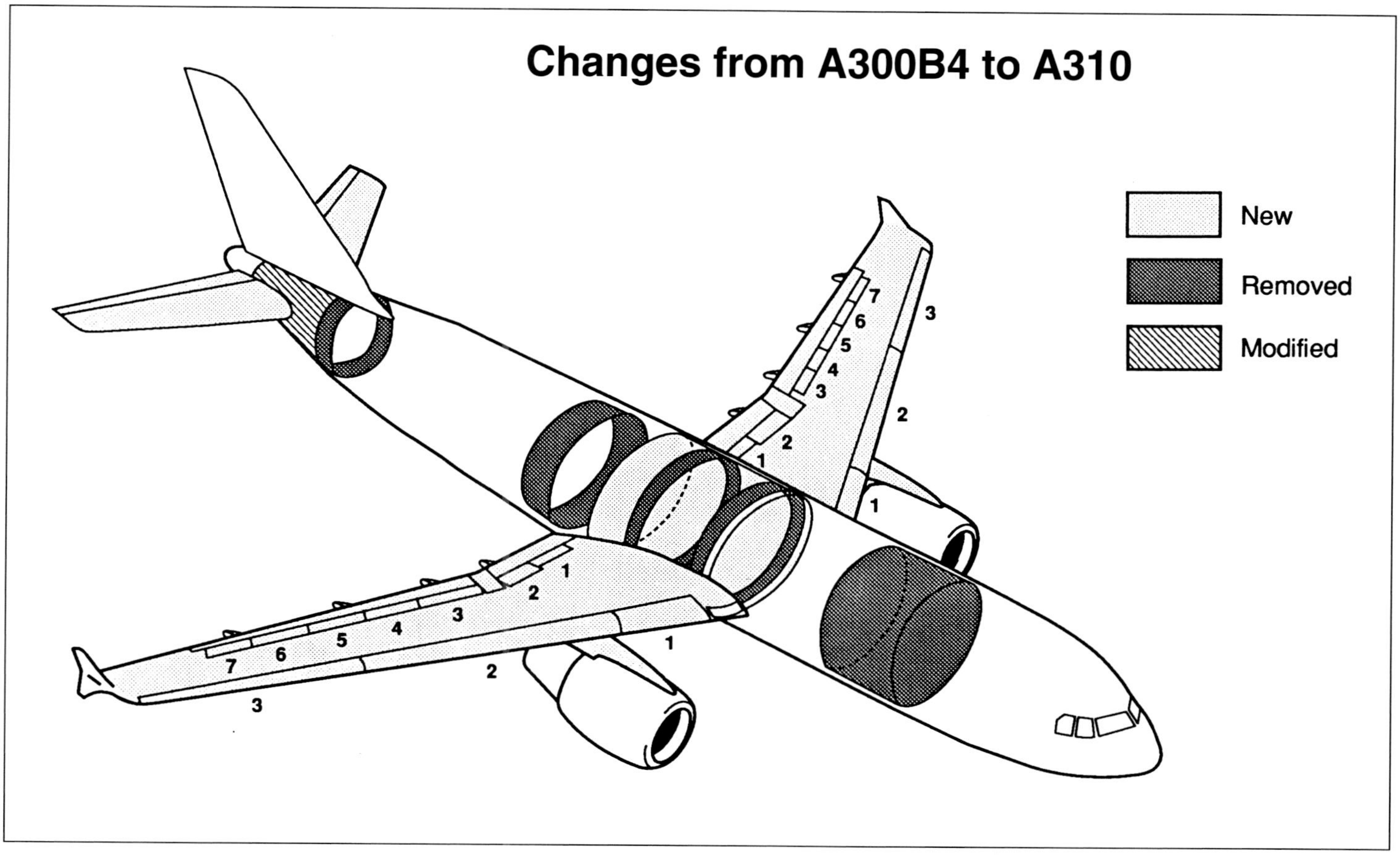
Changes from A300B4 to A310
New
Removed
Modified
1
2
3
4
5
6
7
1
2
3
4
5
6
7
1
2
3
1
2
3

	A310-300	A310-300	A310-300	A310-300	A310-300
Max operating altitude	12,500m	12,500m	12,500m	12,500m	12,500m
	41,000ft	41,000ft	41,000ft	41,000ft	41,000ft
Take-off field length	2,410m	2,550m	2,485m	1,753m	1,753m
	7,910ft	8,365ft	8,155ft	5,750ft	5,750ft
Landing field length	1,480m	1,480m	1,630m	1,555m	1,555m
	4,855ft	4,855ft	5,350ft	5,100ft	5,100ft
Range with typical payload	4,300nm	4,300nm	5,150nm	4,350nm	4,350nm
	7,955km	7,955km	9,530km	8,050km	8,050km
	4,940miles	4,940miles	5,920miles	5,000miles	5,000miles

External dimensions	A310-300	A310-300	A310-200F*	A310-300F*	A310-300F*
Wingspan	43.90m	43.90m	43.90m	43.90m	43.90m
	144 ft 0¼in	144 ft 0¼in	144 ft 0¼in	144 ft 0¼in	144 ft 0¼in
Length overall	46.67m	46.67m	46.67m	46.67m	46.67m
	153ft 1½in	153ft 1½in	153ft 1½in	153ft 1½in	153ft 1½in
Height overall	15.81m	15.81m	15.81m	15.81m	15.81m
	51ft 10½in	51ft 10½in	51ft 10½in	51ft 10½in	51ft 10½in
Tailplane span	16.26m	16.26m	16.26m	16.26m	16.26m
	53ft 4¼in	53ft 4¼in	53ft 4¼in	53ft 4¼in	53ft 4¼in
Max fuselage diameter	5.64m	5.64m	5.64m	5.64m	5.64m
	18ft 6in	18ft 6in	18ft 6in	18ft 6in	18ft 6in
Wheel track	9.60m	9.60m	9.60m	9.60m	9.60m
	31ft 6in	31ft 6in	31ft 6in	31ft 6in	31ft 6in
Wheelbase	15.21m	15.21m	15.21m	15.21m	15.21m
	49ft 10¾in	49ft 10¾in	49ft 10¾in	49ft 10¾in	49ft 10¾in

	A310-300	A310-300	A310-200F*	A310-300F*	A310-300F*
Internal dimensions					
Main cabin length	33.25m	33.25m	33.25m	33.25m	33.25m
	109ft 1in	109ft 1in	109ft 1in	109ft 1in	109ft 1in
Max cabin width	5.28m	5.28m	5.28m	5.28m	5.28m
	17ft 4in	17ft 4in	17ft 4in	17ft 4in	17ft 4in
Max cabin height	2.33m	2.33m	2.33m	2.33m	2.33m
	7ft 7¾in	7ft 7¾in	7ft 7¾in	7ft 7¾in	7ft 7¾in
Areas					
Wing, gross	219m²	219m²	219m²	219m²	219m²
(sq ft)	2,358	2,358	2,358	2,358	2,358
Leading-edge slats	28.54m²	28.54m²	28.54m²	28.54m²	28.54m²
(sq ft)	307.2	307.2	307.2	307.2	307.2
Krüger flaps	1.12m²	1.12m²	1.12m²	1.12m²	1.12m²
(sq ft)	12.0	12.0	12.0	12.0	12.0
Trailing-edge flaps	38.68m²	38.68m²	38.68m²	38.68m²	38.68m²
(sq ft)	516.4	516.4	516.4	516.4	516.4
Ailerons	6.86m²	6.86m²	6.86m²	6.86m²	6.86m²
(sq ft)	73.84	73.84	73.84	73.84	73.84
Spoilers	7.36m²	7.36m²	7.36m²	7.36m²	7.36m²
(sq ft)	79.22	79.22	79.22	79.22	79.22
Airbrakes	6.16m²	6.16m²	6.16m²	6.16m²	6.16m²
(sq ft)	66.31	66.31	66.31	66.31	66.31
Fin	45.24m²	45.24m²	45.24m²	45.24m²	45.24m²
(sq ft)	486.9	486.9	486.9	486.9	486.9
Rudder	13.57m²	13.57m²	13.57m²	13.57m²	13.57m²
(sq ft)	146.1	146.1	146.1	146.1	146.1
Tailplane	64m²	64m²	64m²	64m²	64m²
	689sq ft	689sq ft	689sq ft	689sq ft	689sq ft

	A310-300	A310-300	A310-200F*	A310-300F*	A310-300F*
Elevators	19.20m²	19.20m²	19.20m²	19.20m²	19.20m²
	206.7sq ft	206.7sq ft	206.7sq ft	206.7sq ft	206.7sq ft

Accommodation

Passengers (typ/max)	220/280	220/280	220/280	220/280	220/280
Cargo volume	102.1cu m	102.1cu m	312.1cu m	312.1cu m	312.1cu m
	3,605cu.ft	3,605cu.ft	11,023cu.ft	11,023cu.ft	11,023cu.ft

Power plant

Number and type	2 x PW4156A	2 x PW4156A	2 x CF6-80C2A2	2 x CF6-80C2A2	2 x PW4152
Thrust (each)	249.2kN	249.2kN	238.1kN	238.1kN	231.4kN
	56,000lb	56,000lb	53,500lb	53,500lb	52,000lb

Weights and loadings

Max take-off weight	164,000kg	164,000kg	142,000kg	153,000kg	157,000kg
	361,555lb	361,555lb	313,050lb	337,305lb	346,120lb
Max landing weight	124,000kg	124,000kg	123,000kg	124,000kg	124,000kg
	273,370lb	273,370lb	271,165lb	273,370lb	271,165lb
Max zero-fuel weight	114,000kg	114,000kg	113,000kg	114,000kg	114,000kg
	251,325lb	251,325lb	249,120lb	251,325lb	251,325lb
Operating weight empty	81,545kg	82,270kg	72,400kg	73,900kg	73,900kg
	179,775lb	181,490lb	159,615lb	162,920lb	162,920lb
Max payload	32,455kg	31,730kg	40,600kg	39,100kg	40,100kg
	71,550lb	69,950lb	89,505lb	86,200lb	88,405lb
Fuel capacity	61,070kg	68,270kg	54,920kg	61,070kg	61,070kg
	134,635lb	150,510lb	121,077lb	134,635lb	134,635lb

Performance

Max permitted operating speed (Vmo)					
	340kts	340kts	340kts	340kts	340kts
	629km/h	629km/h	629km/h	629km/h	629km/h
	391mph	391mph	391mph	391mph	391mph
Max operating speed (Mmo)	Mach 0.84	Mach 0.84	Mach 0.84	Mach 0.84	Mach 0.84
Typical cruise speed	457kts	457kts	457kts	459kts	459kts
	845km/h	845km/h	845km/h	849km/h	847km/h
	525mph	525mph	525mph	527mph	527mph
Approach speed	135kts	135kts	135kts	135kts	135kts
	250km/h	250km/h	250km/h	250km/h	250km/h
	155mph	155mph	155mph	155mph	155mph
Max operating altitude	12,500m	12,500m	12,500m	12,500m	12,500m
	41,000ft	41,000ft	41,000ft	41,000ft	41,000ft
Take-off field length	2,360m	2,360m	2,485m	2,550m	2,550m
	7,745ft	7,745ft	8,155ft	8,365ft	8,365ft
Landing field length	1,555m	1,555m	1,630m	1,555m	1,555m
	5,100ft	5,100ft	5,350ft	5,100ft	5,100ft
Range with typical payload	4,800nm	5,250nm	3,100nm	4,050nm	4,800nm
	8,880km	9,710km	5,735km	7,490km	8,880km
	5,515 miles	6,030 miles	3,560 miles	4,650 miles	5,515 miles

Note on Tables

The A310-200 and A310-300 were produced in a number of variations (mainly with different engine choices) which accounts for the four A300-200 and seven A300-300 headings in these tables, all of which have very similar dimensions.

LEFT: The Belgian Air Force acquired two second-hand A310-200s for VIP duties.   * Converted from passenger aircraft

GENERAL DESCRIPTION

The short/medium-range A310 development of the world's first wide-body twin-engined airliner was the result of airline demands for a smaller capacity aircraft, but one with a high degree of commonality with the A300 and taking advantage of newly available technology. Major innovations were a new advanced-technology wing, new and smaller horizontal tail plane, and digital two-crew cockpit.

Initially known as the A300B10 variant when only one of the early options among the Airbus range, the A310 was finally launched in July 1978. In its basic A310-200 version, it was offered with a choice of General Electric CF6-80A3 or Pratt & Whitney JT9D-7R4E1 powerplants, and entered service with Lufthansa on 12 April 1983. Martinair Holland became the launch customer of the convertible A310-200C, delivered to the airline on 29 November 1984. Increased range was provided in the A310-300, which introduced a number of higher take-off weight options and increased fuel capacity. Swissair accepted the first JT9D-7R4E1-powered model on 17 December 1985. Delta-shaped wingtip fences were introduced as standard on the A310-300, and also added on the A310-200, with Thai Airways International taking the first on 29 April 1986. One or two ACTs (Additional Centre Tanks) for extra long range were certificated in November 1987. More powerful CF6-80C2A2 and the new PW4152 turbofan engines had also been added in the meantime, with further engine options introduced from late 1991, including the CF6-80C2A8 and PW4156A. Since 1988, only the A310-300 has been built — German airline Hapag-Lloyd taking delivery of the last A310-200 in March 1988. Although there have been no new customers for the A310 since Uzbekistan Airways took delivery in June 1998, the production line remains officially open.

STRUCTURE

The A310 fuselage is of semi-monocoque, fail-safe construction of circular cross-section, using aluminium alloys with improved stress corrosion and crack propagation behaviour. It is manufactured in nine structural sections (for ease of transportation) largely from sheet metal fabricated frames, open section stringers and skins. In general, the skins are formed from simple sheet metal, except in highly loaded areas such as the centre fuselage at the wings and landing gear and the nose gear bay, where the skins are machined. Except where integrally machined, stringer attachment is by hot bonding or rivetting. The A310 is fitted with a tail bumper beneath the rear fuselage to protect the structure against excessive nose-up attitudes during take-off and landing.

A considerable amount of composites has been introduced, including glass-fibre reinforced plastic (GFRP), aramid-fibre reinforced plastic (ARFP) and carbon-fibre reinforced plastic (CRFP). These are used for floor struts and panels, spoilers, wing leading-edge lower access panels, wing/fuselage fairings, nosewheel doors, glide antenna cover, cooling air inlet fairings, main landing gear doors, flap track fairings and flap access doors, engine cowls and the complete fin box. The A310 was the first production aircraft to be certificated with a composite primary structure, starting with an A310-300 for Swissair in December 1985. A total of 13,670lb (6.2 tonnes) of composite material adds up to a weight saving of 3,090lb (1.4 tonnes) over a conventional metal structure. The fin box itself is 255lb (115kg) lighter and has 95 percent fewer components.

All areas of the fuselage are pressurised, except for the radome, the rear fuselage section (tailcone), the nose landing gear bay and the lower segment of the centre section, which includes the air conditioning, hydraulic and main landing gear bays. Each engine is supported on a pylon, which forms a fail-safe box-type frame, constructed of high tensile steel. The attachment of the pylon to the wing consists of inner and outer triple-lugged titanium forge attachments, with two sets of twin steel links bolted to double lugs and to two pairs of titanium forged fittings attached to the forward face of the front wing spar and the wing skins. A spherical stainless steel bearing transmits longitudinal and lateral loads to a titanium spigot forging bolted through the lower wing skin to the forward attachment fittings. The attachment of the engine to the pylon is via a pyramid-shaped mounting machined from forged steel, which picks up the front spigot of the engine. This spigot transmits longitudinal and lateral loads, while four tension bolts carry the vertical loads.

The A310 wing has a thickness/chord ratio of 10.8 percent and a 28° sweepback and is made up of three main components providing a continuous and fail-safe two-spar box structure with machined skins and I-section stringers. It is built mostly of high-strength aluminium alloy, except for the spoilers, outer shrouds, flap track fairings, flap access doors, leading edge lower access panels and wing/fuselage fairings, which are of composite materials. The centre wing box is built integrally into the fuselage, to which are attached the port and starboard cantilevered outer wing sections.

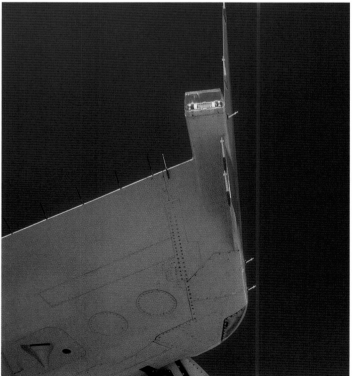

ABOVE: Close-up of underwing fairings.

FAR LEFT: Close up of General Electric CF6-80C2 turbofan engines, one of two powerplants used on the A310.

LEFT: Rear view of wingtip fence.

BELOW: Drag-reducing winglets were introduced with the A310-300, but were also retrofitted to earlier A310-200s.

Movable surfaces on the leading edge include three slats on each wing, two outboard and one inboard of the engine, with a Krüger flap at the wing root. Trailing edge devices comprise a single Fowler flap outboard, vaned Fowler flap inboard, an all-speed aileron mounted behind the engine, and three spoilers, two outer speed brakes/spoilers and two inner speed brakes on the upper trailing edge surfaces of each wing forward of the flaps. All 14 can be used as lift dumpers. A highly swept delta-shaped wingtip fence has been added for reduced cruise drag of up to 1.5 percent.

The original reduced size horizontal stabiliser on the A310-200 was further redesigned with the introduction of a trim tank system in the A310-300, which is now fitted to all versions ('dry' in the –200 and 'wet' in the –300 model). The structure is composed of a main box, removable leading edges with reinforced forward portions for hail and bird impact protection, rear shroud panels, two elevators and a tip fairing. All rear elements are of composite construction.

The main box structure is made up of three parts, a centre and two outer boxes made of integrally machined panels, spars and spar webs. The ribs in the centre box are also integrally machined, while in the outer boxes, the ribs are either designed with web plates or struts. The fin comprises a main box, a removable leading edge, rear shrouds, a tip, and a single rudder, constructed almost entirely from composite materials. The lightning strike zone area of the torsion box has a GFRP outer skin used as a dielectric coating for enhanced protection. The removable leading edge, as on the tailplane, is divided into four span-wise sections for ease of handling and interchangeability. The forward skin is also covered with a special paint to prevent erosion. The stabilisers are actuated by fail-safe ball screwjack, which can be electrically or mechanically controlled.

The life of the primary structure has been designed to meet three main objectives: structural endurance without fatigue cracks is 17,500 flights or 30,000 hours; structural endurance in normal operating conditions, possibly with minor cracks but no replacement of large parts is 23,000 flights or 40,000 hours; and structural endurance with economic repairs is 35,000 flights or 60,000 hours. The crack-free life of the landing gear is 50,000 flights.

POWERPLANT

The A310 is in service with high bypass turbofan engines from both major US manufacturers (General Electric and Pratt & Whitney) fitted on underwing pylons. By design, the engines equipped with accessories and system components are identical for right-hand and left-hand applications. This also applies to the nose cowl, primary nozzle and plug. Fan cowls and fan reverser halves are interchangeable on the same engine position, while pylon and pylon fairings are interchangeable on the same aircraft position.

While the initial A310-200 models were offered with the 48,000lb (213.5kN) thrust Pratt & Whitney JT9D-7R4E1 and 50,000lb (222.4kN) General Electric CF6-80A3 engines, both

ABOVE RIGHT: The Pratt & Whitney PW4000 series engine was introduced on the A310 from 1986.

BELOW RIGHT: Trim tank in lower rear cargo hold.

BELOW: Thrust reverser operating principle on the PW engine.

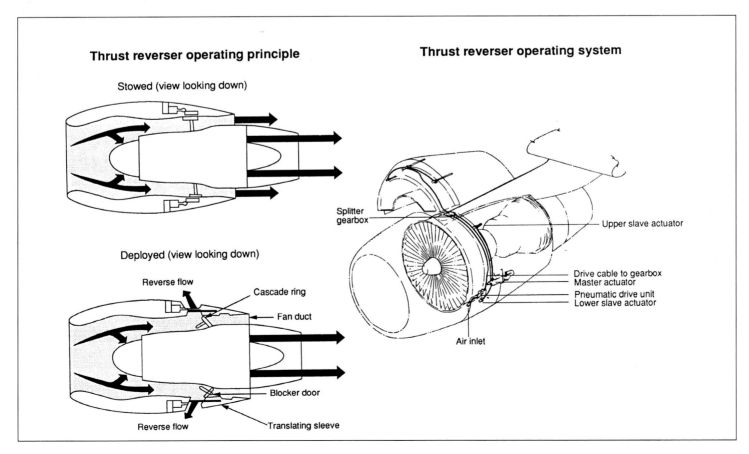

Thrust reverser operating principle

Stowed (view looking down)

Deployed (view looking down)

Reverse flow
Cascade ring
Fan duct
Blocker door
Translating sleeve
Reverse flow

Thrust reverser operating system

Splitter gearbox
Upper slave actuator
Drive cable to gearbox
Master actuator
Pneumatic drive unit
Lower slave actuator
Air inlet

the A310-200 and A310-300 were later fitted with the more powerful 53,500lb (238.1kn) CF6-80C2A2 and 52,000lb (231.4kN) PW4152 turbofans. Still more power and improvements were made available from late 1991 with the 59,000lb (262.5kN) CF6-80C2A8 and 56,000lb (249.2kN) PW4156A engines.

The CF6-80C2 was a complete re-design of the earlier CF6-50, providing a higher thrust range from 59,000lb (262.5kN) to 61,500lb (273.7kN), and lower specific fuel consumption (SFC) and improved EGT margins. The advanced derivative has a larger fan case with a 93in (2,362mm) diameter fan and blades with better bird strike resistance. A fourth booster stage has been added to the LP compressor, while improvements in the 14-stage HP compressor aerodynamics cut down internal losses. The LP turbine has retained the proven 80A3 flow path, but another rotor stage has been added by introducing an additional 5th stage and aerodynamically shaping the struts of the rear frame to match with increased fan and booster requirements. The engine retains the aluminium/Kevlar fan blade containment shroud and noise suppression panels in the fan case of the 80A3.

The 56,000lb (249.2kN) thrust Pratt & Whitney JT9D-7R4 is more powerful than earlier JT9D engines and features a larger single-stage fan with 40 wide-chord blades (compared to 46 in the –59A), a four-stage LP compressor, improved combustor, single-crystal HP turbine blades, increased diameter LP turbine, and electronic supervisory fuel control.

The third-generation PW4000 series, as well as providing still higher thrust (58,000lb/258.1kN in the PW4158), is distinguished by a seven per cent reduction in SFC and improved maintainability through simplified construction. Other features are a 93in (2,362mm) diameter fan, single-crystal turbine blades, aerodynamically-enhanced aerofoils, 'plug-in' modules, a more efficient Thermatic rotor, and FADEC (Full Authority Digital Engine Control).

The earlier CF6-80A3 featured an accessory drive gear box mounted externally on the fan case for ready access and a cool environment, but the later CF6-80C2, JT9D-7R4 and PW4000 series introduced a core-mounted gear box for cleaner aerodynamic lines and a more compact nacelle geometry. The three new-technology engines are also notable for a considerable improvement in noise attenuation through the use of composites in the nacelle and engine — with the associated weight savings. Smoke and emission levels have also been lowered. Air for starting the engine is supplied through a pneumatic manifold from an external high-pressure source, the onboard APU, or by cross-feed from the opposite engine.

Reverse thrust is provided by a cascade fan reverser system for each engine, actuated by pneumatic drive motors powered by engine compressor bleed air or pneumatic system air. The system of one engine is completely independent of the opposing engine. The fan reverser consists of translating sleeve blocker doors and fixed cascades, the latter tailored to generate effective retarding forces and to minimise exhaust gas re-injection at lower speeds. In the stowed position, the system forms a passage for the fan stream flow to the exhaust fan; while deployed,

it provides reverse thrust, with thrust modulation being accomplished by power setting adjustments. The fan reverser is powered by one drive unit for both reverser halves, fed with air from the 15th stage supply (PW) or the ECS supply (GE). Maximum thrust is permitted down to 60kts IAS. After inadvertent deployment in flight up to 300kts IAS, it is possible to re-stow the thrust reverser below 250kts IAS at 24,500ft (7,500m) altitude.

FUEL SYSTEM

Fuel capacity has been progressively increased through the A310 family range. Fuel in the initial A310-200 model is stored inside the wing box, which is divided into five separate tanks. The centre tank contains 5,188US gal (19,640l), the two inner wing tanks hold 3,684US gal (13,945l) each, and the two outer wing tanks 976US gal (3,695l) each, giving a total capaci-

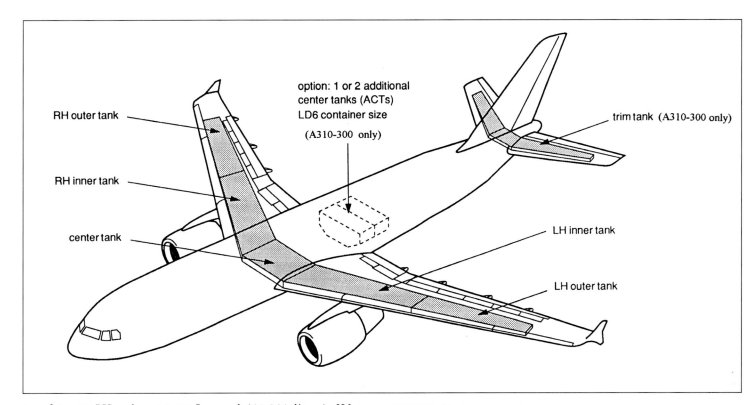

RH outer tank

RH inner tank

center tank

option: 1 or 2 additional
center tanks (ACTs)
LD6 container size

(A310-300 only)

trim tank (A310-300 only)

LH inner tank

LH outer tank

ABOVE: Fuel tank arrangement.

RIGHT: The A310 cockpit was designed with the help of car manufacturer Porsche to provide a comfortable and efficient environment.

ty of 14,491US gal or 12,097Imp gal (54,920 litres). Water drainage is provided at the low points of each tank and can be performed with up to 2° ground slope. All tanks are equipped with manholes to provide access to the interior. The A310-300 has a 1,623US gal or 1,355Imp gal (6,150l) fuel tank in the horizontal stabiliser, bringing total capacity to 16,114USgal or 13,452Imp gal (61,070 litres). In addition to increasing the air-craft's range, the computerised fuel transfer system in the trim tank also provides active centre of gravity (c.g.) control for more efficient production of lift. The net result is a 1.5 percent reduction in cruise drag and lower fuel burn. One or two ACTs (Optional Additional Centre Tanks) in the aft rear cargo hold of the A310-300 can increase total fuel capacity to 19,913US gal or 16,623Imp gal (75,470 litres). The usable fuel volume is 1,902US gal (7,200l) in each tank. The ACTs are fed to/from the centre wing tank, with parallel refuelling if both tanks are installed in 45 minutes. Removal/installation of the ACTs can be accomplished overnight.

The fuel system is designed for single-point refuelling/defuelling control by one operator from a panel located under the fuselage centre section. Two standard two inch fuelling adaptors are provided under the leading edge of the right hand wing, outboard of the engine, enabling a com-plete refuel from empty in 24 minutes. Normally, each engine is supplied with fuel pumped from its own wing by three-phase AC booster pumps mounted two per tank for fail safety, but cross-feed and transfer valves permit fuelling of both engines to be fed from one side, or all the fuel to be used by one engine. Each pump can dry-run for about 15 minutes.

In an emergency, the wing tanks can be refuelled by gravi-ty via one over-wing filler point per tank. The tanks are used in the order — centre, inner, outer — with the outer wing tank pumps fitted with sequence valves, so that fuel from these tanks can only be used if there is no supply from the centre or inner tanks. Refuelling of the centre tank can be done by trans-fer of fuel from the wing tanks using the aircraft fuel pumps. Defuelling is carried out either by the use of the tank booster pumps or through suction. No jettison system is fitted on the Airbus. A surge tank to collect any fuel spilt from the vent pipes during ground or flight manoeuvres is contained in each wing tip. The trim tank in the A310-300 has its own surge tank located at the right hand extremity of the tail plane.

FLIGHTDECK

The A310 flightdeck was planned and designed with the aid of stylists from the Porsche luxury car manufacturer, to produce a spacious and ergonomically-styled interior, with crew comfort and low workload the prime considerations. Central to these aims were separate environmental controls for cool fresh air selection, providing reduced crew fatigue and, therefore, improved operational safety; invisible smoker/non-smoker cen-tre line separation through ventilation; high level of automa-tion; automatic switching or change-over; 'lights out' concept; and a centralised warning system.

From the outset, accommodation was provided for two crew members — captain and first officer — with an additional observer seat behind and on the centre line. A rear left folding jump seat for occasional use is an option. Crew stations, instru-ment panels, control column and rudder pedals were designed for optimum seat positions and visibility. The window enclo-

sure (comprising two large front panes, two sliding lateral direct vision panes and two fixed lateral rear vision panes,) provides excellent rearward vision to the wing tips. The forward down vision cut-off angle is 18.5°. All windows are electrically heated to prevent icing on the front panels and misting up of the side panels. The front panels are heated by a conductive gold film, which minimises optical distortion. The avionics compartment below the flightdeck can be accessed via a trap door.

The pilots' instrument panels contain all primary flight and navigational instruments, while the centre panel incorporates those instruments where joint-use is acceptable, such as the primary engine instruments, the master warning panel, the

brake pressure indicator, and the standby attitude, airspeed and altitude instruments. Flap/slat indicators and landing gear controls are positioned closer to the first officer. Flightdeck features include an EFIS (Electronic Flight Instrument System), an ECAM (Electronic Centralised Aircraft Monitor) unique to Airbus, digital avionics and flight management systems. Six 6.25 x 6.25in interchangeable CRT (cathode ray tube) displays are used for primary flight, navigation and warning information.

The EFIS comprises a primary flight display (PFD) and navigation display (ND) mounted vertically for each pilot, while there are two ECAM displays, warning (WD) and systems (SD), in the lower centre position. Display can be selected

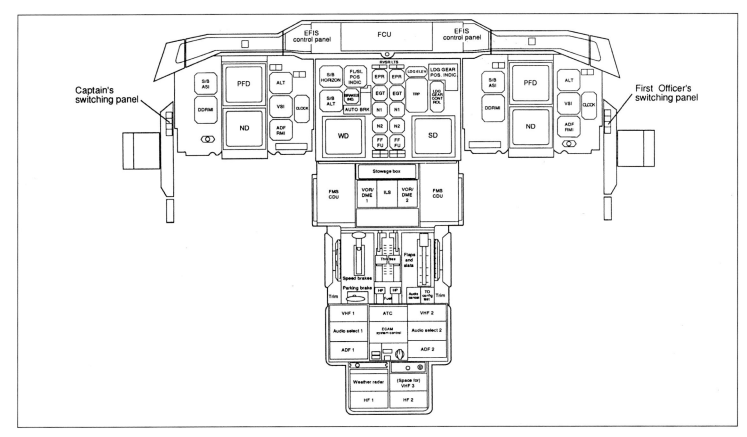

Captain's switching panel

First Officer's switching panel

ABOVE: Main instrument panel and pedestal.

ABOVE RIGHT: Primary flight display

BELOW RIGHT: Flight control surfaces.

LEFT: Outer wing showing roll spoilers and outboard flaps.

BELOW: Overhead instrument panel.

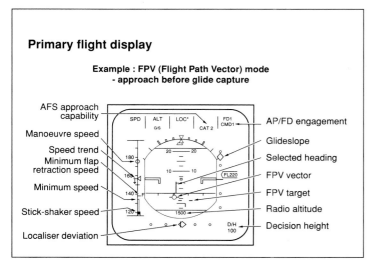

Primary flight display

Example : FPV (Flight Path Vector) mode
- approach before glide capture

AFS approach capability

Manoeuvre speed

Speed trend
Minimum flap retraction speed

Minimum speed

Stick-shaker speed

Localiser deviation

AP/FD engagement

Glideslope

Selected heading

FPV vector

FPV target

Radio altitude

Decision height

FLIGHT CONTROLS AND GUIDANCE

The A310 flight controls consist of primary and secondary systems. The primary flight controls comprise ailerons, roll spoilers, trimmable horizontal stabilisers, elevators and rudder, while the secondary flight controls consist of full-span three-section leading edge slats, trailing edge cambered tabless flaps, and roll spoilers and speed brakes, all of which can be used as lift dumpers. The primary flight controls are mechanically controlled and fully powered by three independently supplied hydraulic servo-jacks, with no operational reduction after a single hydraulic failure. The tailplane is actuated by a fail-safe ball screwjack driven by two independently controlled hydraulic motors, which are electrically controlled with an additional mechanical input.

The primary systems provide attitude control in pitch, yaw and roll. Pitch control and trim is achieved by two elevators hinged on the horizontal stabiliser, each actuated by three servo-jacks controlled by a dual mechanical linkage. A duplicated artificial feel system creates load feel at the column, which is variable with flight conditions. An autopilot actuator is located adjacent to the left hand elevator. It provides control via a detent lever, which can be overridden by the crew.

A stick-shaker (electric motor) is installed on each control column, to provide stall warning to the crew. Pitch trim is achieved by adjustment of the horizontal stabilisers, either manually by trim wheel operation, or automatically by autopilot trim, Mach trim or alpha (angle of attack) trim functions. Electrical and automatic trim signals are processed by two FACs (Flight Augmentation Computers), which control two electric motors. Elevator and horizontal stabiliser positions are indicated on the right ECAM display unit.

to appear on different CRTs. Two FMS (Flight Management Systems) represent the main means of navigation (automatic), which can be overridden through the FMS-CDU (Control Display Unit). There is also an air data system with two DADC (Digital Air Data Computers) and three IRS (Inertial Reference Systems), plus a standby. In the case of a failure of one DADC, switching allows the recovery of altitude, speed, Mach and static air temperature information from the remaining DADC.

The central pedestal layout affords easy access to both crew members. Forward of the throttles are the navigation controls, while alongside the throttles are the controls for the flaps/slats, speed brakes and trim wheels, with the fuel levers and parking brake located just behind. At the rear are the audio controls, VHF communications, and ADF (Automatic Direction Finder).

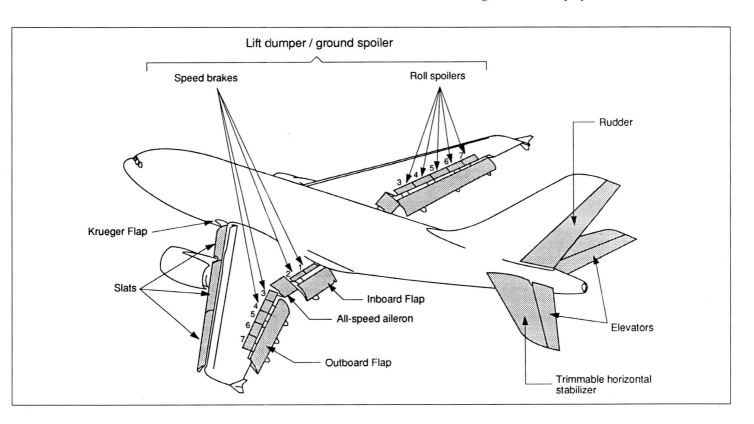

Lift dumper / ground spoiler

Speed brakes

Roll spoilers

Rudder

Krueger Flap

Slats

Inboard Flap

All-speed aileron

Outboard Flap

Elevators

Trimmable horizontal stabilizer

For roll control, the A310 has on each wing one all-speed aileron mounted behind the engine, powered by three servo-jacks, and five roll spoilers, each powered by one servo actuator. All are operated by the pilots' control wheels through a spoiler servo and mixer assembly. An auto pilot actuator is attached to the right hand wing rear cable quadrant, which is again controlled via a detent lever and can be overridden by the crew.

The aileron trim control is electrically powered, and the roll spoilers are electrically signalled by two identical digital computers, designated EFCU (Electronic Flight Control Unit). Yaw control is provided by a single-piece rudder, which is operated by three independently-supplied, mechanically-controlled servo-jacks. The rudder receives pilots' input from the pedestal mechanism by a single cable run up to a spring-loaded artificial feel unit, connected to the trim screwjack. Commands are delivered by two independent rudder travel channels of the FLC (Feel and Limitation Computers), which receive inputs from the ADC (Air Data Computer) and SFCC (Slat/Flap Control Computers).

There are two inner and two outer speed brakes located on the upper surface of each wing, controlled by single servojacks, supplied by different hydraulic systems. The outer speed brakes are also used as lift dumpers/roll spoilers and are selected by a lever situated on the pedestal. Speed brake and roll spoiler surfaces are used on the ground as ground spoilers, being automatically extended after touch-down when specific conditions are fulfiled.

High-lift control on each wing is achieved by three leading edge slats, continuous across the engine pylon, and a Krüger flap, in conjunction with single Fowler flap outboard, vaned Fowler flap inboard, and drooped all speed ailerons. The all speed ailerons droop down to 10° to maintain flap continuity in the region of the engine efflux. The Krüger flaps are provided to complete the wing leading edge profile when the slats are extended and to obtain better aerodynamic characteristics. The flaps are operated by individual hydraulic actuators. Each flap and slat surface is driven by two ball screwjacks. Two identical SFCCs (Slat Flaps Control Computers) provide continuous monitoring of the high-lift control system.

All models of the A310 are equipped with a digital AFS (Automatic Flight System). This has been designed to provide cruise guidance with fail soft characteristics; approach guidance with fail passive characteristics to permit Cat II automatic approach and landing and Cat I normal approach; approach guidance with with fail operational characteristics to permit Cat IIIb automatic approach and landing; and flight augmentation with fail operational capability by duplication of the system. At the heart of the system are two FCC (Flight Control Computers) for flight director and autopilot functions; a single TCC (Thrust Control Computer) for speed and thrust control; two FAC (Flight Augmentation Computers) to provide yaw damping, electric pitch trim and flight envelope monitoring and protection; and two FMC (Flight Management System Computers) for position computation, navaids auto-tuning, flight plan construction and lateral and vertical guidance along the flight plan. Options are improved availability of speed and

thrust functions with a second TCC, and a transfer switch to allow crosstalk of FMS CDU and ND after one FMC failure.

The FCC takes care of the FD (Flight Director) and the CMD (Autopilot in Command Mode) or in CWS (Control Wheel Steering) mode. The FD is permanently engaged. Only one autopilot can be engaged at any one time, except during the automatic landing and go-around phases. The crew disconnects the autopilot by depressing the instinctive disconnect push button on the control column. The TCC computes the engine limit parameters, simultaneously processing the maximum operational value (limit) and the recommended value (target).

The autothrottle operates in three modes: automatic angle-of-attack protection when the throttle is in the armed phase; a speed (speed or Mach)/thrust mode (N1 or EPR); and a 'thrust latch' mode, which provides full thrust when selected either manually or automatically. The FAC provides yaw damping, electric pitch trim and flight envelope protection.

ELECTRICAL AND PNEUMATIC POWER

Power generation is identical on both A310 variants. The A310 has a 115V 400Hz AC system and a 28V DC system. In normal flight conditions, basic AC power comes from the two compact and lightweight 90kVA engine-driven IDGs (Integrated Drive Generators) or a third auxiliary generator driven by the APU. Any one of the three generators is capable of providing all the AC power up to 90kVA if the other two fail. In the case of power loss from all three generators, three batteries or a hydraulically driven AC/DC standby generator can supply emergency power for a minimum of 30 minutes, to allow a safe landing with reduced radio and navigation equipment.

On the ground, the entire aircraft network can be supplied either from the APU or the ground power unit, with the latter having priority. The primary sources for DC power are three TRU (Transformer/Rectifier Units), and three 25Ah Ni/Cd batteries for emergency supply and APU starting.

The AlliedSignal (Garrett) GTCP 331-250N self-contained APU (Auxiliary Power Unit), installed in the tailcone aft of the cabin pressure bulkhead, is designed to provide bleed air to the aircraft pneumatic system and to drive an oil-spray cooled AC generator during ground and in flight operations.

Independence from external sources on the ground (up to 8,500ft/2,590m) is assured by power available to drive a 90kVA oil-spray cooled AC generator, and additionally to supply bleed air for main engine start or air conditioning system. During flight operation, the APU is capable of providing either electrical power (over the whole flight envelope), or to supply bleed air for emergency wing anti-icing, including air conditioning through one pack. It can also provide starter assisted engine relights or air conditioning by two packs respectively, up to 20,000ft (6,100m). Maximum operating limit of the APU is 41,000ft (12,500m).

The APU is supplied with fuel through a separate fuel line, drawing fuel from the left hand main engine system, but can be fed from any tank when the cross feed valve is open. A dedicated APU pump is installed in that line to permit fuel supply to the APU when the engine fuel system is not operating. A shut-off valve on the tank boundary permits isolation of the APU fuel line when the APU is cut off, to avoid pressure on the fuel line across the pressurised zone. A second shut-off valve is installed upstream of the APU firewall to allow for fuel cut off in an emergency. The APU fuel control system is fully automatic and controlled and monitored by the ECB (Electronic Control Box) installed in the pressurised rear fuselage.

The A310 pneumatics supply HP (High-Pressure) air to the air conditioning and pressurisation, wing anti-icing, engine starting, potable water tank pressurisation, hydraulic reservoirs and the rain repellent system. HP air is supplied from different stages of the engine's compressors, the APU load compressor, or from two standardised 3in (76mm) ground connections. Two independent systems use bleed air from each engine to supply the thrust reverser and engine intake air ice protection. A third system is installed for the ventilation of the wing leading edge inboard of the engine, using a ram air inlet. No monitoring or manual control is provided.

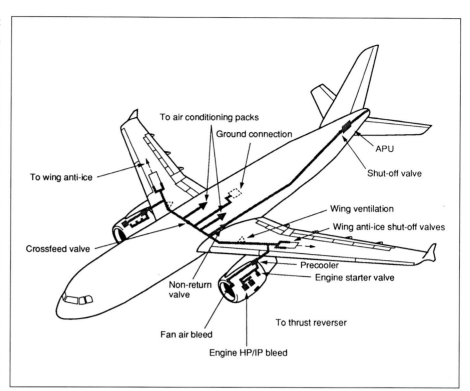

ABOVE: Pneumatic system layout.

BELOW: Electrical power generation and distribution control.

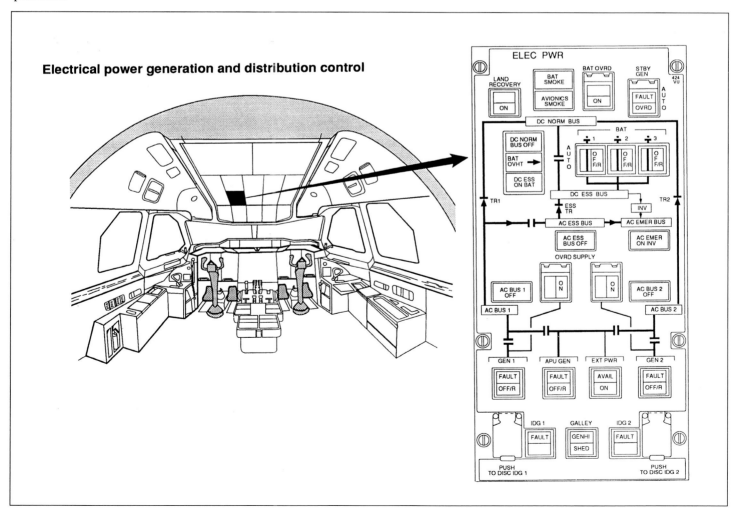

Electrical power generation and distribution control

AIR CONDITIONING AND PRESSURISATION

The air conditioning system serves four independently controlled zones in the aircraft: the flightdeck and three passenger cabins, with the forward and rear areas including galleys and toilets. Airflow routing also provides ventilation of the avionics compartment and the lower cargo holds. In the A310 air is supplied to the toilets and galleys from an individual ventilation system, with cabin pressure differential providing extraction during the flight, while a fan is used when the aircraft is on the ground.

Hot air is tapped downstream of the bleed air control valves and supplied via a pneumatics distribution manifold to two air conditioning packs, located under the central wing box and accessed via the main landing gear well. Each pack incorporates a three-wheel 'bootstrap' air cycle machine with an air-to-air heat exchanger, where the air is cooled and routed, via a common manifold, to the four zones. Temperature control is achieved automatically or manually by varying the pack outlet temperature and adding trim (hot) air. The air supply can also be taken from the APU, and conditioned air can be supplied directly to the cabin air distribution system by two low-pressure ground connections. A ram air inlet is provided for fresh air ventilation in flight when the packs are not operating. The proportion of fresh air to recirculated air in normal mode is between 60 percent and 40 percent.

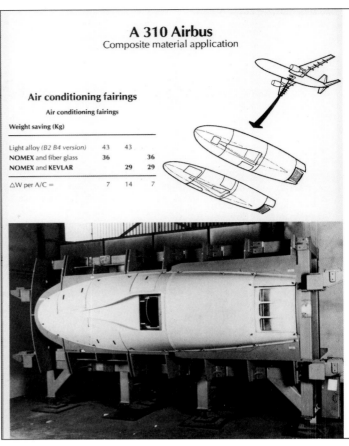

A 310 Airbus
Composite material application

Air conditioning fairings

Air conditioning fairings

Weight saving (Kg)

Light alloy (B2 B4 version)	43	43
NOMEX and fiber glass	36		36
NOMEX and KEVLAR		29	29
△W per A/C =	7	14	7

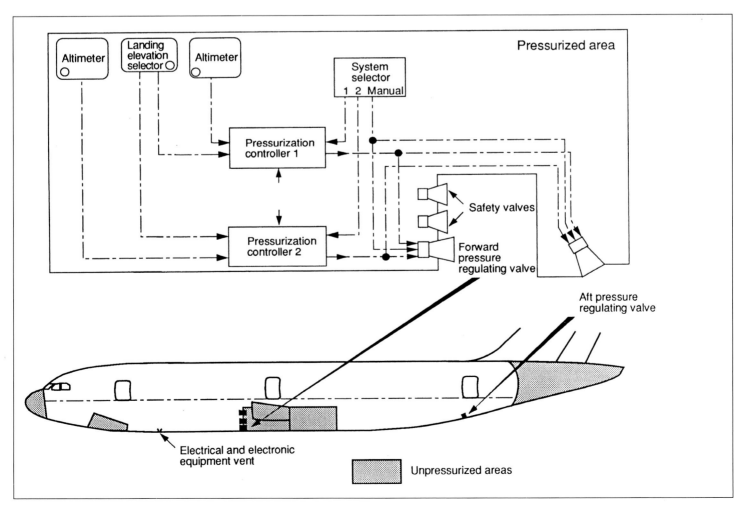

48

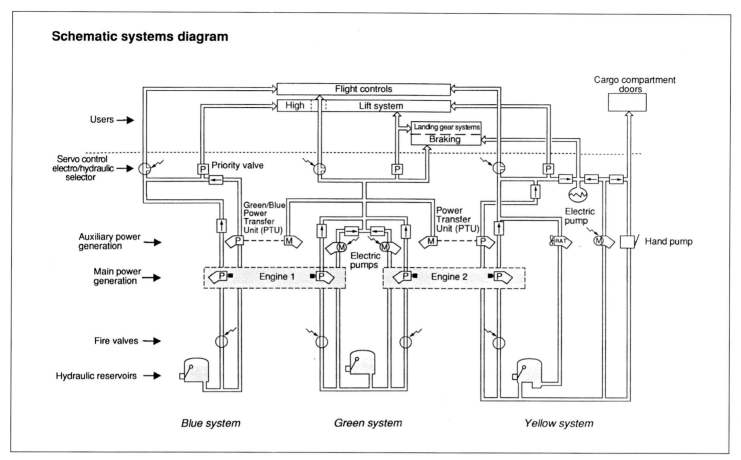

Schematic systems diagram

ABOVE: Hydraulic system schematic diagram.

ABOVE LEFT: Kevlar reinforced air conditioning fairings under the central wing box are 14kg lighter than aluminium and 7kg lighter than glassfibre.

LEFT: Cabin pressure control system.

Pressurised areas in the A310 are the flightdeck, passenger cabin, avionics compartment and cargo holds.

Control is provided by two electric outflow valves, one situated forward of the air conditioning bay, the other aft of the bulk cargo compartment, operated by two independent automatic cabin pressure systems, one active and the other stand-by. Switch-over from one to the other is automatic after each flight, and in the case of failure of the active system. Manual control of the outflow valves is possible by switches in the overhead panel. Ground depressurisation is achieved automatically by electrically opening the outflow valves. Automatic pre-pressurisation of the cabin before take-off is provided to prevent a noticeable pressure fluctuation in the cabin during rotation on take-off.

HYDRAULIC SYSTEM

The hydraulic system operates the fully powered flight controls, landing gear and braking system, and the cargo compartment doors. It comprises three parallel, fully independent systems, each pressurised by at least two independent means, to ensure aircraft control in the event of the loss of two systems or both engines. Each includes a reservoir and is pressurised to 3,000lb/sq in (207bars).

The main power generation consists of four identical variable displacement pumps driven by the engine accessory gearboxes. Auxiliary power is provided by two electric pumps for use mainly on the ground for maintenance and check list purposes, two power transfer units in the event of failure of the LH or RH engines or on the ground, a pump driven by ram air turbine should both engines fail, an electric pump pressurising the braking accumulator and allowing cargo compartment door operation on the ground. A hand pump is also available for emergency operation of the cargo doors. The flight control servos are protected against high flow consumers by priority valves.

LANDING GEAR

The landing gear on both A300 models is of conventional hydraulically actuated tricycle-type, with two four-wheel tandem mounted bogies on the main unit and twin-wheels on the nose gear. A tail bumper has been incorporated to protect the rear aircraft structure in the event of a high nose-up attitude during either take-off or landing. The main gears are located under the wing and retract sideways towards the fuselage centreline, while the nosewheel unit retracts forward into the fuselage. In the extended position, the main gear is braced laterally by foldable side struts, and the nose gear by a telescopic drag strut. The nose gear steering system is hydraulically powered with mechanical control.

Normal operation of the gears is by hydraulic operating jacks. Gear extension and retraction sequences are electrically initiated by command signals from a three-position lever

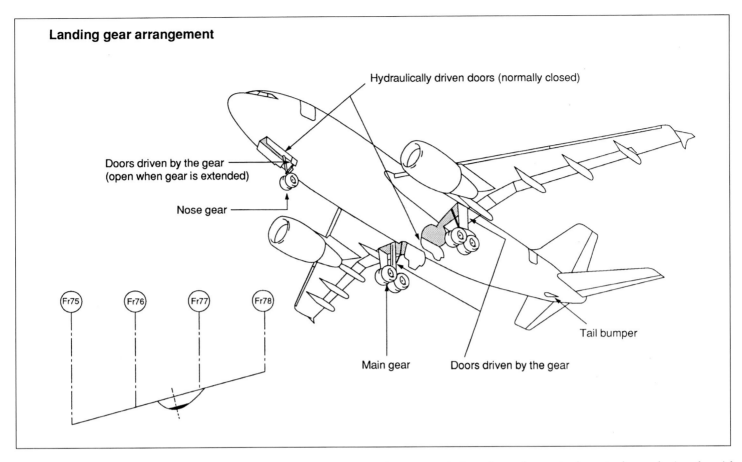

Landing gear arrangement

Hydraulically driven doors (normally closed)

Doors driven by the gear (open when gear is extended)

Nose gear

Fr75 Fr76 Fr77 Fr78

Main gear

Doors driven by the gear

Tail bumper

ABOVE: Landing gear arrangement.

BELOW: The main landing gear comprises two four-wheel bogies.

(up–neutral–down) on the central control panel. A solenoid operated anti-retraction latch is installed to prevent the normal gear control lever being moved to the up position, unless shock absorber struts are fully extended and the nose wheels and main bogie beams are perpendicular to the gear leg. Emergency extension of the nose and main gears is possible by manual release of the uplock mechanism and free fall extension and locking of the gears, with automatic spring assistance for the main gear and aerodynamic load for the nose gear. Visual and aural indicating and warning systems alert the crew when the landing gear is not locked down during approach.

A mechanical alternative means of checking that the gear is locked-down is provided by a red pin protruding on each wing upper skin above the gear well, which is visible from the cabin. Nose gear down-lock can be ascertained through a viewer located in the avionics compartment, even in the event of adverse environmental conditions, such as misting, frosting or water accumulation.

The eight wheels of the main landing gear are equipped with a multi-disc carbon brake, each with an anti-skid system based on slip ratio control. This permanently compares the braked wheel speed with the actual aircraft speed, in order to control the braked wheel speed to a pre-determined slip ratio. Brake temperature indication and overheat warning is provided on the flightdeck. Protection against tyre skidding and locked-wheel touchdown is also built in. Automatic braking and the installation of brake cooling fans are optional.

Normal braking pressure is controlled by one master valve per main landing gear, and supplied to the eight brakes via

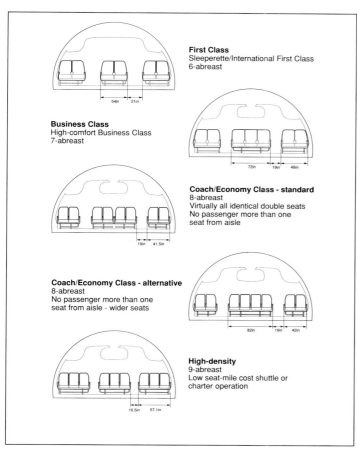

First Class
Sleeperette/International First Class
6-abreast

Business Class
High-comfort Business Class
7-abreast

Coach/Economy Class - standard
8-abreast
Virtually all identical double seats
No passenger more than one
seat from aisle

Coach/Economy Class - alternative
8-abreast
No passenger more than one
seat from aisle - wider seats

High-density
9-abreast
Low seat-mile cost shuttle or
charter operation

ABOVE: Passenger cabin adaptability.

ABOVE RIGHT: Overhead stowage.

BELOW RIGHT: A310 First class cabin.

BELOW: Typical cabin layouts.

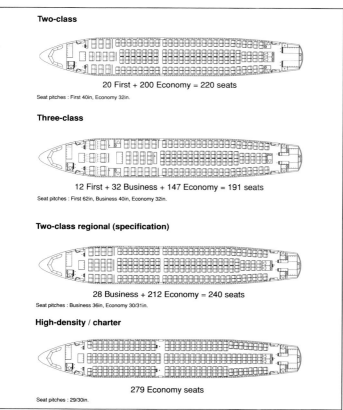

Two-class

20 First + 200 Economy = 220 seats

Seat pitches : First 40in, Economy 32in.

Three-class

12 First + 32 Business + 147 Economy = 191 seats

Seat pitches : First 62in, Business 40in, Economy 32in.

Two-class regional (specification)

28 Business + 212 Economy = 240 seats

Seat pitches : Business 36in, Economy 30/31in.

High-density / charter

279 Economy seats

Seat pitches : 29/30in.

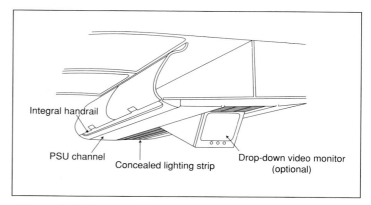

Integral handrail

PSU channel

Concealed lighting strip

Drop-down video monitor
(optional)

eight anti-skid servo valves. Emergency braking is supplied by the second hydraulic system via an accumulator, but anti-skid protection is not available. The main landing gear wheels and brakes are furnished by Messier-Bugatti.

CABIN INTERIORS AND CARGO HOLDS

The 18½ft (5.64m) fuselage cross-section provides an optimum balance between aerodynamic considerations, true wide-body passenger accommodation, and a standard underfloor cargo systems fit. It allows customised twin-aisle layouts, ranging from a six-abreast first class configuration to nine-abreast high-density seating for the charter market. A typical mixed-class layout in the A310 accommodates 20 first class passengers in a 2/2/2 configuration with a 40in (102cm) seat pitch, plus 200 economy class passengers 2/4/2 at 32in (81cm) pitch, narrowing to 2/3/2 in the rear fuselage taper. A three-class configuration could accommodate 12 first class (62in [157cm])

seat pitch, 32 business (40in) and 147 economy seats (32in). High-density nine-abreast charter seating is possible for up to 280 passengers. Some 95 percent of passenger seats are double-seat units with a width of 40.4in.

There is a gap between the two centre units to ensure that each passenger has at least one armrest not shared with another passenger. The two aisles in economy class are 19in (48cm) wide. Attendant seats are also incorporated, one at each door, and a purser station in the front passenger cabin. Two optional attendant seats can be installed at the front side of the forward cabin bulkhead.

The cabin has been designed for four galleys, with a total capacity of 21 trolleys, allowing the serving of two hot meals plus beverages. The standard aircraft is equipped with five lavatories, four in the rear and one in the forward cabin. Structural provisions have been made for an additional lavatory in the front cabin.

Access to the cabin is via four large doors along each side of the fuselage, two ahead of the wing and two at the rear, measuring 42 x 76in (1.07 x 1.93m x 1.07m). These are outward parallel-opening plug-type doors and require no power assistance. They are impossible to open in normal cruise flight with the aircraft pressurised. There are also two 26½ x 53in (0.67 x 1.34m) plug-type emergency exits of similar construction over the wings, and two 24 x 28in (0.7 x 0.6m) crew emergency exits.

The A310 has two underfloor cargo compartments, which can accept all standard ULD (Unit Load Devices) in current use. In the forward hold, up to eight LD3 or four LD6 containers can be carried two-abreast, while three full-size pallets or a mixture of both are alternative options. The rear hold can take up to six LD3 or three LD6 containers plus bulk cargo. A net separates the rear cargo from the bulk cargo compartment, which has a usable volume of around 610 cu.ft (17.3m³) and a load capacity of 6,100lb (2,770kg). All the holds can be heated and ventilated so that livestock can be carried.

Access to the main cargo compartments is provided by two doors in the lower right hand side of the fuselage. The forward door measures 106 wide x 67in high (2.7m x 1.7m), and the rear hold door 71 wide x 67in high (1.81m x 1.7m). Both doors open outwards and upwards hydraulically, with manual locking/unlocking, and extend over the full height of the holds. There is also a manually-operated 37½ x 37½in (0.95m x 0.95m) plug-type door to the bulk cargo compartment. The A310-200C convertible and A310-200F and -300F freighter conversions, have a main deck cargo door on the forward left hand side with 70° or 145° opening angle and measuring 141in wide x 101in high (3.58m x 2.57m). Typical cargo on the main deck of the A310F comprises 16 88in x 125in (223.5cm x 135.5cm) or 18 88in x 108in (223.5cm x 274cm) pallets in side-by-side loading, or five containers and five pallets.

Both the forward and aft cargo compartments can be provided with a semi-automatic electrically powered loading sys-

BELOW: Business class service in the A310.

ABOVE: Economy class in a Lufthansa A310

tem, which is controlled by an operator from the control panel, located behind service doors in the outer skin on the right hand side of each doorway. The system permits manual loading/unloading if the power drives are inoperative.

PROTECTIVE SYSTEMS AND EMERGENCY EQUIPMENT

A fire protection system provides immediate detection of a fire in the engine nacelles and APU compartments through aural and visual indications, together with extinguishing components. The electronic bay is provided with a smoke detection system, while the cargo compartments comprise both smoke detection and fire extinguishing equipment. Lavatories are also provided with smoke detection and an automatic waste bin fire extinguishing system. Additionally, portable fire extinguishers are installed in the avionics bay, on the flightdeck and in the passenger cabin. The detection system consists of two parallel sensing loops in each protected area, both of which must be subjected simultaneously to fire or overheat conditions before triggering the alarm, thus reducing the risk of false warnings. The fire extinguishing system for each engine nacelle consists of two extinguisher bottles installed at the rear part of the pylon, while one bottle is provided for the APU. Smoke in the avionics bay is detected by four self-contained smoke detectors of the ionisation type, with two detectors provided per cargo compartment. For fire extinguishing in the cargo holds, two bottles, each equipped with two independent discharge cartridges, are installed in the forward cargo compartment.

The A310 is also provided with two independent emergency oxygen systems, one for the flight crew and one for cabin staff and passengers. The systems have been designed for three flight profiles, including a one-minute delay at maximum altitude, nine minutes descent to 10,000ft (3,050m), and 65 minutes continuation of flight at or below 10,000ft for the crew. The gaseous low-pressure system for the crew includes quick-donning masks with mask-mounted regulators and smoke goggles, fed from a 76.5ft^3 (2.7m^3) rechargeable pressure bottle. For the passengers, a solid-state system (a drop-out continuous flow system installed in the overhead racks and including oro-nasal masks) was chosen for ease of installation, safety and reduced weight.

An emergency evacuation signalling system enables the flight or cabin crew to warn each other and the passengers by warning lights and an audio tone. The system can be operated from a panel on the flightdeck, at the purser's station and from the C/A station aft of the rear left hand door. Other emergency equipment distributed through the cabin includes fire extinguishers, axes, megaphones, flash lights, radio beacons, therapeutic portable oxygen bottles and masks, and life jackets sufficient for passengers, crew and demonstration purposes.

All emergency egress is through the cabin doors, but the flight crew also has the option of using the 28in x 24in (0.7m x 0.6m) sliding windows, for which escape ropes are provided. The forward and rear passenger doors are equipped with double-track escape slides, while the mid-cabin emergency exits

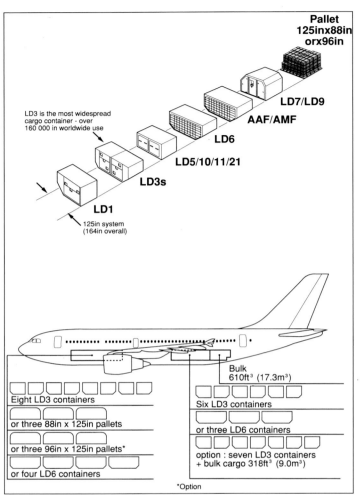

LD3 is the most widespread cargo container - over 160 000 in worldwide use

Pallet 125inx88in orx96in

LD7/LD9

AAF/AMF

LD6

LD5/10/11/21

LD3s

LD1

125in system (164in overall)

Bulk 610ft³ (17.3m³)

Eight LD3 containers

or three 88in x 125in pallets

or three 96in x 125in pallets*

or four LD6 containers

Six LD3 containers

or three LD6 containers

option : seven LD3 containers + bulk cargo 318ft³ (9.0m³)

*Option

have single-track slides. On overwater equipped aircraft, slides on doors one, two and four are replaced by a slide/raft combination, configured to function as slides in a ground evacuation, and as rafts when detached from the aircraft following a ditching. Emergency lighting is provided for the passenger areas and the external surrounds of the exits, powered from the 28V DC supply and/or the 6V emergency Ni/Cd batteries.

Ice and rain protection for critical areas of the aircraft permits unrestricted operation in icing conditions and heavy rain. Ice protection is achieved by hot air or electrical heating. The hot air anti-icing system includes the outboard part of the leading edge slats of each wing totalling some 47.5 percent of the aircraft span, engine air intakes, and the engine itself (Pratt & Whitney only). The front windshield panels and side windows in the cockpit, sensors, pitot probes and static ports, and the waste water drain masts are electrically heated. Rain from the front windshield panels is cleared by wipers and, when necessary, by a rain repellent fluid system.

Ice protection bleed air for the wing is taken from the engine or APU via the crossfeed duct and controlled by two shut-off valves and restrictors in each wing. When no engine bleed air is available for wing protection, the APU can be used. Engine anti-ice is provided for the P&W engine only by hot air bled from the eighth stage compressor to the first stage stator vanes. For both P&W and GE engine nacelles, each nacelle is provided with an intake anti-ice system.

LEFT: Cargo hold flexibility.

BELOW: Wing anti-ice system.

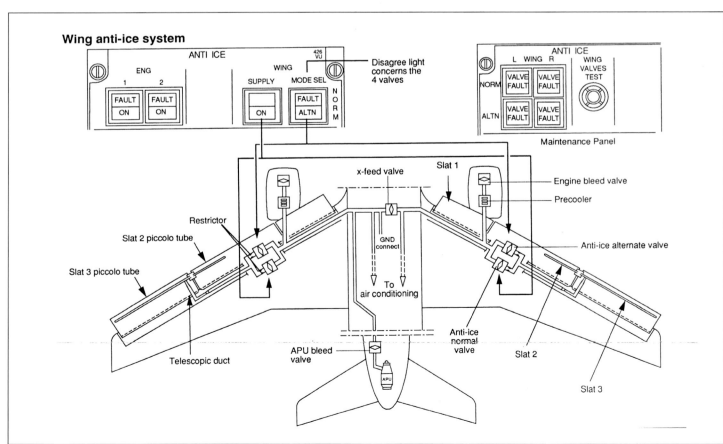

Wing anti-ice system

ANTI ICE

ENG
1 2

WING
SUPPLY MODE SEL

426 VU

FAULT ON FAULT ON   ON   FAULT ALTN   N O R M

Disagree light concerns the 4 valves

ANTI ICE
L WING R   WING VALVES TEST

NORM VALVE FAULT VALVE FAULT

ALTN VALVE FAULT VALVE FAULT

Maintenance Panel

x-feed valve

Slat 1

Engine bleed valve

Precooler

GND connect

To air conditioning

Anti-ice alternate valve

Restrictor

Slat 2 piccolo tube

Slat 3 piccolo tube

APU bleed valve

Anti-ice normal valve

Slat 2

Slat 3

Telescopic duct

APU

4 In Service

When launch customers Lufthansa and Swissair took delivery of their first A310-200s in March 1983, they became owners of what was arguably the most advanced airliner in the world. Considering that the manufacturer had broken new ground with the 'little' Airbus, problems encountered by the two airlines in the first six months of operations, were of relatively minor extent. The German flag-carrier put the new type into service on 10 April, when it flew a Frankfurt-Stuttgart sector, followed later that day with a flight to London. As the A310 has a two-crew cockpit, Lufthansa retrained redundant flight engineers, who demonstrated the appropriate aptitude, into pilots. By the summer, the six-strong A310 fleet was to be found on prime domestic services and some international routes, such as Athens, Cairo, Istanbul, London, Moscow, Paris and Vienna. Swissair's first service took place on 21 April, and its fleet served similar European destinations from Zürich and Geneva. At the end of the year, A310s were also in service with KLM Royal Dutch Airlines and Kuwait Airways Corporation, the latter having placed an order for six aircraft on 6 December 1980.

It was perhaps not surprising that Lufthansa and Swissair both encountered some difficulties with the computer hardware and software, although generally, these were minor and did not

require the aircraft to be taken out of service. Faulty wiring, hot spots on printed circuit boards, glitches with software programming, and hydraulic systems leakage were early difficulties, and Lufthansa also had one CRT failure. The autopilot needed some work, and detailed improvements were required on the electronic centralised aircraft monitor (ECAM) system. Maintenance staff struggled somewhat in understanding the highly-advanced and integrated systems, and as a result, technical reliability was not as high as expected, but still reached 97.5% in Lufthansa service after six months operation and the carriage of 400,000 passengers. The airlines were impressed with the responsiveness of Airbus and all items reported had been fixed in a single package by the end of the year. Both airlines said, however, that problems were few in such an advanced aircraft, and held the A310 up as the best-designed aircraft they had put into service.

At the beginning, Airbus had intended to offer two versions of the A310, the A310-100 with a typical range of 2,000 nautical miles (3,700km), and the A310-200, which could carry 210 passengers a distance of 3,000 nautical miles (5,550km). But with no orders for the former, the A310-100 was never built. However, in 1982, Airbus revealed that it was working on a third version with a further extension to the range, and officially launched the A310-300 during the handover of Swissair's first A310-200, when that airline again became the launch customer. The A310-300 introduced a number of higher take-off weight options and increased fuel capacity, provided in an addi-

ABOVE: CASA tests the tailplane trim tank at its Getafe factory prior to the first flight of the A310-300.

LEFT: First A310-300 in final assembly at Toulouse.

tional trim tank in the tailplane, which also provided active centre of gravity control (c.g.) for more efficient production of lift. Highly swept, delta-shaped wingtip fences were added as standard for reduced drag, and these were also adopted on the A310-200 from spring 1986.

Tip fences provide drag reduction by reducing and controlling the cross-flow, weakening the tip vortices, and improving the lift distribution at the tip. The delta planform and geometry ensures that no shock waves form at cruise speed (avoiding wave drag penalties), flow quality remains satisfactory under all conditions, and drag reductions ensue in the low-speed regime as well as in cruise. The A310 wingtip fences provide a cruise drag reduction of up to 1.5 percent.

The first extended-range A310-300, powered by Pratt & Whitney JT9D-7R4E engines, flew on 8 July 1985, and was followed by a General Electric CF6-80C2-powered model on 6 September. Certification of the A310-300 with Pratt & Whitney engines by the French and German authorities was granted on 5 December, and Swissair put the new type into service 11 days later on routes from Geneva and Zürich to points in Africa. Certification with the CF6-80C2 and improved Pratt & Whitney PW4152 engines was obtained in April 1986 and June 1987 respectively. One further development was a still 'longer-legged' A310-300 with one or two additional centre tanks (ATCs) in the cargo holds, bringing fuel capacity to more than 19,800US gal (75,000l), compared to the near 14,500US gal (55,000l) in the original A310-200. This heaviest A310-300

variant received certification in November 1987 and entered service with Canadian charter airline, Wardair. From the following year, due to airline preference for the longer-range versions, only the A310-300 was built, with German holiday airline Hapag-Lloyd taking delivery on 22 March 1988 of the last A310-200 produced.

A310 MODEL DESIGNATIONS

Model	Engines
-203	2 x 222.4kN (50,000lb)General Electric CF6-80C2A3
-221	2 x 213.5kN (48,000lb) Pratt & Whitney JT9D-7R4D1
-222	2 x 213.5kN (48,000lb) Pratt & Whitney JT9D-7R4E1
-304	2 x 238.1kN (53,500lb) General Electric CF6-80C2A2
-308	2 x 262.5kN (59,000lb) General Electric CF6-80C2A8*
-322	2 x 213.5kN (48,000lb) Pratt & Whitney JT9D-7R4E1
-324	2 x 231.4kN (52,000lb) (Pratt & Whitney PW4152
-325	2 x 249.2kN (56,000lb) Pratt & Whitney PW4156A*

* Latest developments of both engines were introduced from 1991

RIGHT: The first extended-range A310-300 with Pratt & Whitney JT9D-7R4E engines Pratt & Whitney-powered A310-300 skims over runway on a low flypast during its maiden flight.

BELOW RIGHT: CSA Czechoslovak Airlines became the first Soviet Bloc airline to operate the A310, taking delivery of two A310-300s in spring 1991.

BELOW: A310-300 on its first flight.

LESSENING THE LOAD

The A310 was the first commercial aircraft to be certificated with a composite primary structure, first applied to a Swissair A310-300 in December 1985 and subsequently introduced as standard on all models. Developed by Messerschmitt-Bölkow-Blohm (MBB) in Germany, the composites fin box, including the rudder and elevators, is constructed from glass-fibre reinforced plastic (GFRP) and a mix of carbon-fibre reinforced plastic (CFRP) and aramid-fibre reinforced plastic (AFRP), producing a 22 percent (256lb/115kg) weight saving over conventional metal construction.

Additionally, composites construction made it possible to achieve a 95 percent reduction in component parts, excluding fasteners. Development of the rudder started in 1977, and after flight tests in the A300 test aircraft, the rudder underwent a two-year operational test in actual service on a Lufthansa A300 starting in 1981.

Prior to that, it had undergone severe temperature and corrosion tests. The rudder spent many days in a climatic chamber under simulated tropical heat, arctic cold and icing conditions, but withstood all elements. Similarly, in long-term corrosion studies, during which it underwent 144,000 simulated flights, no fatigue damage was detected. Even after the introduction of artificial damage and a further 48,000 'flying hours', no increase in damage was reported. As electrical conductivity is low, a lightning protection system had to be incorporated. This was developed and tested by the Institute for Plasma Physics at the Technical University of Hannover, and comprised lightning conductor strips along the rudder's edge and connected to metal parts on the fin.

Other major composites applications on the A310 include floor struts and panels, spoilers and main landing gear doors,

TOP LEFT: French Air Force A310-300 at Nantes-Atlantique. *Günter Endres*

CENTRE LEFT: Luftwaffe took over the three former Interflug aircraft, including this A310-300 *Konrad Adenauer* used for VIP transport.

LEFT: Royal Thai Air Force VIP A310-300 photographed at Hanoi, Vietnam in September 1997. *Günter Endres*

RIGHT: Internal view of Airbus fuselage converted to freighter configuration.

adding up to a total of 13,670lb (6.2 tonnes) of composite material used, giving a weight saving of 3,090lb (1.4 tonnes).

CONVERTING TO FREIGHT

Airbus Industrie was disappointed at the lack of airline interest in the cargo and combi versions of the A310, with Martinair Holland taking delivery of the only A310-200C convertible aircraft with a large forward maindeck cargo door on the left side on 29 November 1984. But the market was being flooded with second-hand Boeing 747s and earlier generation jet aircraft, and Airbus had also been a victim of its own success. The A310s cargo carrying capacity in the passenger model usually proved sufficient on the short routes operated by the airlines, and gave it an edge over competing aircraft. Its two underfloor cargo compartments were designed to accommodate a combined 14 standard LD3 or seven LD6 containers, or a combination of containers and pallets. Additionally, a bulk cargo hold at the rear had a volume of 610ft^3 (17.3m^3).

In the early 1990s, as mid-life A300s and A310s were coming onto the second-hand market and world cargo traffic grew by more than 8 percent per annum, Deutsche Aerospace Airbus (Dasa) developed a passenger-to-freighter conversion kit for both Airbus models. This has proved extremely popular for the older A300s, but also found a large customer for the A310 in small package specialist Federal Express (FedEx), which placed an order for the conversion of 41 aircraft, all early A310-200s taken out of mainline service by such airlines as Lufthansa, KLM and Swissair. The 41 converted aircraft were delivered to FedEx between July 1994 and April 1998. The kit is also available for conversion of the A310-300, but no orders have yet been placed by commercial operators.

Externally visible structural changes in the A310-200F from the passenger aircraft include the addition of a large 141 x 101in (3.58 x 2.57m) main deck cargo door on the port side (as fitted to the convertible C model), and the replacement of the passenger window panes by fire resistant metal plates. Passenger doors are de-activated and permanently blocked. The main deck floor is reinforced to increase running loads, including the addition of new stronger floor panels and new seat tracks. The main deck also has Class E fire protection and sniffer system for smoke detection, a 9g strap-type safety barrier net and smoke curtain. Systems adaptation/simplifications for the freighter role is also standard, and includes removal of all passenger related systems such as air-conditioning, passenger service system, and passenger interior, and adaptation of protective lining, instruments, warning systems and others.

Optional packages include manual or semi-automatic, electrically-powered cargo loading systems on both decks if required, providing either single row, side-by-side or integrated (combined single row and side-by-side) loading, and AMA container loading provisions, making it possible to position five AMA containers on the A310F. Typical capacity is up to 16 main deck 88 x 125in (2.25 x 3.175m) pallets, four pallets underfloor and 11 LD3s, or a total of 23 LD3 unit load devices (ULDs). An optional crew galley module can be installed just aft of the cockpit and forward of the safety barrier, on the right

hand side. The galley has three rearward-facing seats, overhead and side stowage, lighting, oxygen, communication, life vests and other safety equipment. Enhanced payload capability, revised interior linings and weight saving proposals are also available. Conversion work on the A310 has been carried out under the Dasa supplemental type certificate (STC) by Dasa company Elbe Flugzeugwerke in Dresden, and by Aerospatiale Group member Sogerma at Bordeaux and Toulouse, but any qualified modification centre can undertake this work if requested by the customer. Conversion typically takes two 25-man teams a total of 10 weeks to complete.

A310 Freighter /Convertible Conversions (at 1 January 1999)

C/n	Model	Operator	Elbe	Sogerma
0162	A310-222F	Federal Express (FedEx)	*	
0191	A310-203F	Federal Express (FedEx)	*	
0201	A310-203F	Federal Express(FedEx)	*	
0217	A310-222F	Federal Express (FedEx)	*	
0224	A310-222F	Federal Express (FedEx)	*	
0230	A310-203F	Federal Express (FedEx)	*	
0233	A310-203F	Federal Express (FedEx)	*	
0237	A310-203F	Federal Express (FedEx)	*	
0241	A310-203F	Federal Express (FedEx)	*	
0245	A310-203F	Federal Express (FedEx)	*	
0248	A310-203F	Federal Express (FedEx)	*	
0251	A310-222F	Federal Express (FedEx)	*	
0254	A310-203F	Federal Express (FedEx)	*	
0257	A310-203F	Federal Express (FedEx)	*	
0260	A310-222F	Federal Express (FedEx)	*	
0264	A310-203F	Federal Express (FedEx)	*	
0273	A310-203F	Federal Express (FedEx)	*	
0281	A310-203F	Federal Express (FedEx)	*	
0283	A310-203F	Federal Express (FedEx)	*	
0288	A310-222F	Federal Express (FedEx)	*	
0297	A310-203F	Federal Express (FedEx)	*	
0303	A310-222F	Federal Express (FedEx)	*	
0313	A310-222F	Federal Express (FedEx)	*	
0333	A310-222F	Federal Express (FedEx)	*	
0339	A310-222F	Federal Express (FedEx)	*	
0342	A310-222F	Federal Express (FedEx)	*	
0343	A310-222F	Federal Express (FedEx)	*	
0345	A310-222F	Federal Express (FedEx)	*	
0346	A310-222F	Federal Express (FedEx)	*	
0349	A310-203F	Federal Express (FedEx)	*	
0353	A310-203F	Federal Express (FedEx)	*	
0356	A310-203F	Federal Express (FedEx)	*	
0359	A310-203F	Federal Express (FedEx)	*	
0360	A310-203F	Federal Express (FedEx)	*	
0362	A310-203F	Federal Express (FedEx)	*	
0364	A310-203F	Federal Express (FedEx)	*	
0394	A310-203F	Federal Express (FedEx)	*	
0397	A310-203F	Federal Express (FedEx)	*	
0400	A310-203F	Federal Express (FedEx)	*	
0425	A310-304CC	Canadian Armed Forces		*
0434	A310-304MRT	Luftwaffe	*	
0441	A310-304CC	Canadian Armed Forces		*
0444	A310-304CC	Canadian Armed Forces		*
0482	A310-304CC	Canadian Armed Forces		*
0503	A310-304MRT	Luftwaffe	*	
Total			**41**	**4**

Note: Several more FedEx conversions ordered

MRTT : Tanker versions

Probe and drogue

Boom

TOP: **The A310 is targeted at the Multi-Role Tanker Transport (MRTT) requirements of Australia and the UK.**

ABOVE: **A310 Tanker versions can be equipped with wing pod-mounted hose and drogue units, or aft fuselage boom.**

SLIPPING INTO UNIFORM

A number of air forces acquired the A310 as VIP aircraft and troop and/or freight transports. The only one to buy a brand new aircraft was the Royal Thai Air Force, which took delivery of a VIP-configured A310-300 for use by the Royal Flight on 5 November 1991. The Canadian Forces boosted their strategic airlift capability with five ex-Wardair/Canadian Airlines International A310s in 1992/93. Redesignated CC-150 Polaris, the five aircraft were delivered in a 194-seat passenger configuration, but four were subsequently converted by Sogerma in Bordeaux to a passenger/cargo combi layout. This required some 100,000 engineering and production hours, which included a new main deck cargo door, fuselage and flooring reinforcement, a cargo loading system, and a removable bulkhead and smoke curtain to separate cargo and troops. The fifth aircraft remains in a VIP layout. All are operated by 437 Squadron at 8 Wing, Trenton, Ontario, and are used to re-supply Canadian Forces personnel across the world.

Germany's Luftwaffe operates seven CF6-80C2A2-powered A310-300s and is seeking to acquire two more, to bolster its long-range fleet in the face of increasing logistics demands. The creation of a rapid reaction force, a rise in humanitarian operations, and the new tactical training unit in Mexico, are all making additional demands on its resources. The two A310s are expected to replace the two Boeing 707s by the end of 1999, and two of the existing A310s will be modified to tanker transports by 2003. The Luftwaffe acquired its first three aircraft in May 1991 when the former East Germany carrier Interflug ceased operations, and further enlarged its fleet between November 1996 and November 1998 with four ex-Lufthansa machines. Five are operated in VIP configuration, and two as passenger/cargo combi aircraft. All are operated by 1 Squadron out of Cologne.

Two A310-300s are flown by Transport Squadron 3/60 of the French Air Force (Armée de l'Air) out of Paris Charles de Gaulle Airport. Both have 180 minutes ETOPS (Extended Range Twin Operations) and are used primarily as VIP transports. The A310s were bought from Royal Jordanian in November 1993. The Belgian Air Force obtained two second-hand A310-200s from Singapore Airlines in September 1997 and April 1998, also for use as a VIP transports. The Pratt & Whitney-powered aircraft are operated by 21 Squadron on military and government transport duties, as well as international relief flights.

Multi-role proposals

With the order book for the A310 diminishing and tailing off, Airbus Industrie is hoping that a more determined incursion into the military market will provide a lifeline for the A310. Recognising that reduced defence spending will demand future multi-role aircraft, which are capable of simultaneously carrying out air-to-air refuelling (AAR) and transport (AT) operations, Airbus is offering the A310 in MRTT (Multi-Role Tanker Transport) configuration. With the KC-135 in particular nearing the end of its useful life, the demand for replacement tankers will undoubtedly accelerate, and derivatives of

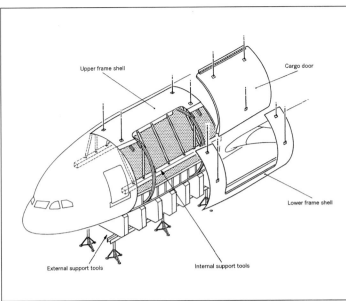

current wide-body aircraft will offer a more cost-effective solution than building a dedicated aircraft from scratch. In addition to offering greater refuelling capacity than earlier airliners, the A310 would also have an advantage in operating costs and longer airframe life. At a price tag in the region of US $30m for a modified second-hand machine, such an aircraft should prove attractive to potential customers. Australia, Canada and Germany are all believed to be in the market for such an aircraft. Airbus studies have indicated a potential market for 100 military tanker/transport aircraft by 2010, of which half are expected to be MRTTs. A demonstrator was produced by the conversion of a former airline A310-300 (N816PA), which undertook compatibility trials with Royal Air Force aircraft in July 1995. No orders had been placed by September 1999.

The A310 MRTT can be converted from existing models or can be new-build aircraft. Powered by the 238.1 kN (53,500lb) General Electric CF6-80C2A2 or 249.2kN (56,000lb) Pratt & Whitney PW4156, the aircraft would have the standard forward port side cargo door of the civil freighter, a quick-change main deck layout, and commonality with existing civil aircraft.

In tanker configuration, the MRTT can be equipped with wing pod-mounted Flight Refuelling Mk 32B-75 hose and drogue units, a rear fuselage boom and central hose drum unit for fuel transfer, to suit individual air force requirements. Fuel is stored in outer, inner and centre wing tanks, a horizontal stabiliser trim tank, and additional underfloor centre tanks, providing a maximum fuel capacity of almost 25,600 USgal/ 21,365Imp gal (97,000l). Some 50 tonnes of fuel can be transferred at 500nm (575 miles/925km), with two hours on station. Fuel transfer is controlled from an operator station using a stereoscopic video system and fly-by-wire controls. Refuelling will take place at speeds between 220 and 320kt (253-368 mph/407-592 km/h).

For transport missions, the main deck can be converted in under 24 hours for up to 279 passengers and troops using palletised seating, or can be configured to carry a variety of pal-

ABOVE LEFT: Artist impression of proposed AEW&C A310.

ABOVE: Conversion of front fuselage to cargo configuration.

ABOVE RIGHT: Cargo being loaded onto a Uzbekistan Airways passenger A310-300.

BELOW RIGHT: A310 in cold water trials at Yakutsk in Eastern Siberia in January 1996. The aircraft was restarted after a 16 hour overnight cold soak in temperatures approaching –50°C. The cloud in the background is condensation in the cold air from the auxiliary power unit (APU) exhaust.

letised and containerised freight. A maximum of 19 88 x 108in (2.25 x 2.75m) pallets can be accommodated in the pure freight role, with 17 possible in a passenger/cargo combi layout. Ten light vehicles can be carried side-by-side on the main deck and in the forward lower cargo compartment. Alternatives include VIP transport, and medevac for 60 stretcher cases plus 32 seats and portable first aid centres, or a combination of all the different possibilities. A self-defence capability can also be built in.

MRTT GENERAL CHARACTERISTICS
External Dimensions
Wing span: 144ft 0¼in (43.90m)
Length (with boom): 155ft 4½in (47.36m)
Length (without boom): 153ft 1in (46.66m)
Height overall: 51ft 10½in (15.81m)
Weights
Max ramp weight: 363,550lb (164,900kg)
Max T-O weight: 361,550lb (164,000kg)
Max landing weight: 273.375lb (124,000kg)
Max zero-fuel weight: 251.325lb (114,000kg)
Max non-fuel payload: 81,570lb (37,000kg)
Max fuel capacity: 170,855lb (77,500kg)
Performance
Max range standard fuel: 4,800nm (5,523 miles/ 8,889km;)
Max range using transferable fuel: 7,200nm (8,285 miles/13,334km;)

WEDGETAIL COMPETITION

The Raytheon Aircraft Systems Division, teamed with Ansett Australia, selected the A310-300 as the platform for its bid for the Australian Airborne Early Warning & Control (AEW & C) requirement, known as Wedgetail, for which it competed with the Boeing 737 and Lockheed Martin C-130J. Airbus was to provide design and engineering support, with Raytheon responsible for the overall system integration and total system performance and certification. Elta Electronic Industries of Israel was to have provided the Phalcon 360° phased-array radar with over 190nm (218 miles/350km) detection range, to be installed in a fixed dorsal dome. The Phalcon provides a high probability of detection, multiple simultaneous modes of operation, close control, and rapid target revisit times.

The mission system also included an open architecture Airborne Tactical Data System; multi-function, dual-display operator workstations; and an Electronic Support Measure (ESM). All systems would be fully interoperable with US and NATO systems. The planned mission duration without refuelling is greater than 10 hours. The Australian requirement was formally announced in January 1997 and a decision was made in July 1999 for the Boeing 737. The Royal Australian Air Force (RAAF) also has a requirement to replace its Boeing 707 tanker fleet, and Airbus may have more luck with the MRTT.

THE END OF THE LINE?

Since the beginning of the 1990s, only 12 new orders have been placed for the A310, the last in 1997. Although the production

line remains open, partially in anticipation of military orders, it would be optimistic to expect further sizeable commercial contracts. With just 261 built, it could not be fairly described as a commercial success story on its own. But in combination with its larger contemporary, the A300 (520 ordered by September 1999), it offered customer airlines a family of aircraft, to which newer types extending capacity both upwards and below the A310, have since been added. The A310 took a decisive lead with advanced technology and helped to give the European Airbus consortium an edge over the competition. It will remain in mainline service for many years to come.

LEFT: In October 1994, an Emirates A310 became the first Airbus aircraft to be fitted with a fax machine.

RIGHT: A310-200 being converted to cargo by Dasa company Elbe Flugzeugwerke in Dresden.

BELOW: Singapore Airlines has become a prolific Airbus operator.

5 AIRLINE OPERATORS

AEROFLOT RUSSIAN INTERNATIONAL AIRLINES

Russia's principal international airline now operates a total of 10 A310-300s on main services from Moscow. The first five, all new A310-300s, were delivered between 30 June and 11 December 1992, although Aeroflot lost one in a highly-publicised crash on 23 March 1994 when, according to the subsequent investigation, the pilot handed control of the aircraft to his son. Four ex-Delta aircraft were added in July and August 1996, followed by two more, once operated by Canadian Airlines, in 1998. Two other A310s were leased for a few months in 1995.

AEROLINEAS ARGENTINAS

The Argentine national flag-carrier began A310 operations in July 1994 when it leased an ex-Delta Air Lines A310-300 for services from Buenos Aires to regional destinations. Two more ex-Delta aircraft followed in August, with a fourth joining the fleet in July 1995. Two remain in service, the others having been returned to Airbus Industrie by 1998. Fitted out for 24 club class and 170 economy class passengers, the A310s are scheduled to points in the Americas, including Bogotá and Los Angeles.

AEROPOSTAL

This long-established and now privatised Venezuelan airline began international services to the United States and regional services within South America in July 1998, following a re-assignment of international routes after the demise of VIASA. It took delivery of an A310-300 in July 1998, and acquired a second in August, which fly the routes from Caracas to Miami, Lima, Santiago, Havana, Santo Domingo and others. Both aircraft are leased from Airbus and are operated in a two-class layout for 198 passengers.

AIR AFRIQUE

A mixed order placed on 21 April 1979 included two A310s, but these were later changed for more A300s. It was not until the early 1990s that this Ivory Coast-based multi-national carrier went back to the smaller Airbus, taking delivery of four

ABOVE RIGHT: Aerolineas Argentinas A310-300.

RIGHT: Air Afrique A310-300.

BELOW: Aeroflot A310-300.

new A310-300s between 29 April 1991 and 11 August 1993. Two more, previously operated in China, were leased from November and December 1994 until their return a year later. The A310s operated on regional routes within West Africa and to Bordeaux, Marseille and Paris in France, but all four were repossessed in July 1998 when the airline found itself in financial difficulties. However, one ex-Oasis A310-300 was leased again on 30 September 1998.

AIR ALGERIE

Algeria's flag-carrier became the 48th Airbus customer on 30 May 1984 when it signed a contract for two A310-200s for its European routes. Both aircraft were delivered later that same year, entering service on the Algiers-Paris route. On 15 January 1988, Air Algerie acquired the two ex-Libyan Arab Airlines A310-200s, but these have been on sub-lease to Royal Jordanian since July 1994 and August 1995. The two A310s link the capital Algiers with Paris and African points such as Bamako, Cairo and Ouagadougou, fitted out for 216 passengers in a two-class configuration.

AIR CLUB INTERNATIONAL

This Canadian charter airline based at Montreal-Mirabel operated for less than four years. It began flying tourists to destinations in Canada, Europe and the Caribbean on 17 June 1994, using an ex-Delta A310-300 delivered two days previously. A

second Delta aircraft was added on 23 September that same year. Apart from charters, the two A310s also flew sub-services for other airlines until financial difficulties forced the airline to cease operations in December 1997. Plans to restart have so far not materialised.

AIR FRANCE

Although it had supported Airbus from the beginning with the A300, Air France was slow to sign up for the A310, mainly through pressure from its pilots' unions, which at first objected to the new two-crew cockpit. It became only the fifth carrier to order the A310 when it signed a firm order for five on 9 May 1979, with options for a further 10 aircraft. The pilots forced a reconfiguration of the flight deck, which delayed first deliveries to 27 April 1984. The last of the five arrived in Paris on 12 April 1985, and were followed by two more A310-200s, delivered in 1986 and 1988. Four more options were taken up later, but changed to the A310-300 model. The fleet now numbers 12 A310s (another A310-300 was acquired in July 1997), which are used primarily on its African routes. One was leased

RIGHT, ABOVE AND BELOW: Two Air France A310-200s.

BELOW: Air Algerie A310-200.

to Air Inter between May and August 1988. Charter subsidiary Air Charter leased two A310-300s for the 1997/98 winter period.

AIR-INDIA

India's international airline added to its three A300s on 8 April 1985 with an order for six A310-300s, the first of which entered service on the Bombay-Muscat route on 20 August 1986. The six aircraft, the first to be powered by General Electric CF6-80C2A2 turbofans, were delivered between April 1986 and March 1987, and were joined by two more in August 1990. Another two were operated on short-term lease from Caribjet during 1994. The eight remain in service on major domestic trunk routes, and international services to such destinations as Abu Dhabi, Dar-es-Salaam, Dubai, Hong Kong, Jakarta, Kuala Lumpur, Kuwait, Manchester, Muscat, Nairobi, Rome, Singapore and Vienna. They are fitted out for 210 passengers in a two-class layout.

AIR JAMAICA

Soon after privatisation on 15 November 1994, Jamaica's national carrier selected an all-Airbus fleet to replace older types. This included six Pratt & Whitney-powered A310-300s,

LEFT: Air India A310-300.

BELOW LEFT: Air Jamaica A310-300.

BELOW: Air Liberté A310-200. *Luis Rosa*

which arrived in Kingston between October 1995 and October 1996. All six are being leased from the manufacturer, having previously been operated by Delta Air Lines. Fitted out for 218 passengers in a two-class layout, the Pratt & Whitney PW4152 and PW4156-powered A310s ply the routes to London, and to North America, where they serve Chicago, Los Angeles, New York-Newark, Baltimore Washington, Philadelphia, Orlando, Ft Lauderdale and Miami.

AIR LIBERTÉ

French independent carrier Air Liberté operated three A310s in the 1990s. Its first A310-200, which was also the first A310 produced, entered service on 30 May 1990, while the second, this time a brand-new A310-300, was delivered on 20 June 1995 and the third, another second-hand A310-200 joined the fleet in January 1996. All were leased from ILFC and operated principally the airline's domestic trunk routes until the last service between Toulouse and Paris on 29 September 1996.

AIR MALDIVES

The national carrier of the Republic of Maldives has leased an ex-Sabena A310-300 from Airbus Industrie Financial Services for a period of three years, starting in November 1997. Flown in a 220-seat configuration with 20 in first class and 200 in economy, the A310 links the capital Malé with Abu Dhabi, Colombo, Dubai and Trivandrum.

AIR NIUGINI

The Papua New Guinea carrier acquired an A310-300, which had been used by Airbus in the certification programme for the Pratt & Whitney PW4000 turbofan engine. It was delivered on

27 January 1989 and commenced revenue flying on the Port Moresby–Singapore route, configured for 30 business class and 179 economy class passengers. The A310 was also used to reintroduce the service to Hong Kong on 20 March. An order was placed for a second aircraft on 10 August that year, for delivery in December 1990. The A310s operate to Brisbane, Hong Kong, Manila, Osaka, Singapore and Sydney.

ARMENIAN AIRLINES

The Armenian flag-carrier began its fleet modernisation programme in mid-1998 with the lease of a second-hand Pratt & Whitney-powered A310-200. The acquisition of the A310-200, delivered on 6 July 1998 and leased from the manufacturer, is part of a plan to move to an all-Airbus fleet by 2005, which could include up to 10 A310s. The 194-seat aircraft is used on the airline's European services from Yerevan to Amsterdam, Frankfurt, Istanbul, London and Paris. Long-haul flights are under consideration.

AUSTRIAN AIRLINES

The Austrian flag-carrier originally ordered two A310-200s for its European routes on 28 May 1980, but changed to the -300 version as soon as it became available, amid good prospects for the resumption of long-haul flights out of Vienna. The two aircraft were handed over on 16 December 1988 and 27 January 1989, and began operating the Vienna––New York and Vienna–Moscow–Tokyo routes respectively on 26 March and 16 July 1989. The Tokyo route was then the longest route served by the A310. Austrian Airlines took delivery of two more, one each in spring 1991 and 1992, and the A310s now serve the routes to New York, Almaty, Astana, Dubai, Male and Kathmandu, with additional winter schedules from Vienna to Luxor, Hurghada, Tenerife, Las Palmas de Gran Canaria and Colombo. Charters are also flown.

ABOVE RIGHT: Air Niugini A310-300.

RIGHT: Austrian Airlines A310-300.

BELOW RIGHT: Armenian Airlines A310-200. *Dennis Norman*

BELOW: Air Maldives A310-300.

BANGLADESH BIMAN

The Bangladeshi flag-carrier is one of the newest A310 operators, having placed an order for two A310-300s on 31 January 1995. Delivery took place on 17 and 19 August 1996. The A310s are scheduled on routes from the capital Dhaka to Abu Dhabi, Bangkok, Calcutta, Dubai, Kuala Lumpur, Kuwait, Muscat, Singapore and Tokyo, fitted out with 25 club class and 196 economy class seats.

BRITISH CALEDONIAN AIRWAYS

The UK's 'second force' airline was an early customer for the A310, signing up for three firm A310-200s and three options on 29 October 1979. It took delivery of the first two on 20 March 1984, which entered service later that month on its Central and West Africa routes, and to Tripoli in Libya. The order for the A310s had originally been placed in response to plans for a large European network expansion, possible Middle Eastern routes, and additional services to North and West Africa. The A310s were also earmarked for B.Cal's proposed low-fare Mini Prix services. However, its aspirations were thwarted by political manoeuvrings, which, together with the decline of its

LEFT: Bangladesh Biman A310-300.

BELOW: British Caledonian Airways A310-200.

African markets, left the airline with insufficient medium-haul work for its Airbuses. On of the three aircraft had already been cancelled earlier and the two in service were reluctantly put up for sale in summer 1986 and went to Libyan Arab Airlines.

CHINA EASTERN AIRLINES/CHINA NORTHWEST AIRLINES
The Civil Aviation Administration of China (CAAC) ordered three A310-200s from Airbus on 16 April 1985, and followed up with an add-on contract for two A310-300s on 7 May 1986. All five were delivered between 25 June 1985 and 28 August 1987, operating domestic and regional trunk services until transferred to Shanghai-based China Eastern Airlines on 25 June 1988, when the CAAC reorganised the civil aviation structure and set up separate airlines. China Eastern sold the three A310-200s in October 1989, two of which found their way to China Northwest Airlines on 29 April and 4 May 1992. The A310-300s continued operating some trunk routes until withdrawn from use and sold in May 1994.

CSA CZECH AIRLINES
The then Czechoslovak national carrier placed an order for two A310-300s on 4 August 1989, as a first step in its programme of re-equipping its fleet with modern western aircraft. The two

RIGHT: China Eastern A310-300.

BELOW: China Northwest A310-200.

BELOW RIGHT: CSA Czech Airlines A310-300.

aircraft entered service on 12 February and 12 March 1991 and are scheduled on its trans-Atlantic routes from Prague to New York, Montreal and Toronto, and eastwards to Abu Dhabi, Dubai and Bangkok.

CYPRUS AIRWAYS

An order for two A310-200s plus two options was signed on 25 February 1982, to replace its fuel-hungry Boeing 707s, primarily on its prime route to London. Simultaneously with the hand-over of the first aircraft on 16 February 1984, Cyprus Airways ordered a third, and added further to its order book on 28 September that year with a fourth, and its first equipped with the new winglets which had become standard on the type. The A310 first entered service on the London route in March 1984, and is now also scheduled on flights from Larnaca to Birmingham and Hamburg. In Cyprus Airways service, the A310 achieves a daily utilisation of close to 10 hours. It is typically equipped for 28 club-class and 213 economy-class passengers.

CYPRUS TURKISH AIRLINES
(KIBRIS TÜRK HAVA YOLLARI)

The airline of the unrecognised Turkish Republic of Northern Cyprus leased an ex-Lufthansa A310-200 between 20 March and 6 November 1994 for its services to mainland Turkey, before acquiring a similar aircraft from Air France on 21 December that same year. An A310-300 joined the fleet in May 1996 but has since been returned. The single aircraft now services KTHY's route from Ercan to Ankara, Antalya and Izmir, connecting with Turkish Airlines' flights to London. The A310 is configured with 225 seats.

DELTA AIR LINES

The acquisition of Pan Am's assets gave Delta not only access to more trans-Atlantic routes, but also Pan Am's fleet of seven A310-200s and 14 A310-300s, the airline's first aircraft from the European manufacturer, officially transferred on 1 November 1991. These continued to be used across the Atlantic, primarily from New York to such points as Frankfurt, Paris and London, and from Detroit and Miami to London, but did not form part of the airline's long-term fleet strategy. Although it acquired seven new aircraft from Airbus in the second half of 1993 (ordered on 9 March 1992), all were withdrawn from use and stored in 1995. Seven were sold to Federal Express for conversion to cargo, while most others were bought by various companies for onward lease.

EMIRATES AIRLINE

Dubai's new international airline started operations with leased aircraft in October 1995, but one year later on 23 October 1986, placed an order with Airbus for two General Electric-powered A310-300s. Both were delivered in July 1987, enabling Emirates to inaugurate services to Europe, at first linking Dubai to London and Frankfurt. The rapid growth of the airline was reflected in additional aircraft purchases, eventually bringing the A310 fleet to 10 when the final aircraft was delivered on 15 May 1995. One has since been sold, but the remaining nine aircraft, fitted out for 181 passengers (18 in first, 32 in business and 131 in economy classes), continue to serve mostly regional routes to Abu Dhabi, Colombo, Delhi, Istanbul, Jeddah, Karachi, Kuwait, Malé, Muscat, Riyadh and others.

ABOVE LEFT: Cyprus Airways A310-200 in its first markings.

LEFT: Delta Air Lines A310-300.

ABOVE RIGHT: Emirates Airline A310-300.

RIGHT: Cyprus Turkish Airlines A310-200. *Terry Shone*

EUROPEAN ENTERPRISE

Danish charter airline Conair overcame a temporary capacity shortage in the busy summer season with the lease of an A310-200 from Sabena, which served with the airline from 1 May to 1 November 1987. In the last year of its existence, Brussels-headquartered Trans European Airways (TEA) operated two leased A310-300s on worldwide charters and IT-flights. It took delivery on 19 December 1990 and 20 March 1991, but suspended operations the following September. The airline had ordered a fleet of eight new A310-300s on 28 April 1989.

A310s made up the main fleet of Bulgarian airline Jes-Air, which leased three aircraft in 1991/92. The first, an ex-China Eastern A310-200, arrived at Sofia on 10 June 1991, followed by an A310-300 leased from Air Niugini. The third was an ex-TAP A310-300, which joined the fleet in June 1992, but all three had been returned to lessors by 4 December 1992, just prior to cessation of all services in January 1993.

Diamond Sakha Airlines in Russia's Far East, now merged into Sakhaavia, was planning to lease two ex-Delta A310-300s in summer 1994, but took delivery of only one on 16 September, with which it began operations on 18 October, serving such destinations as Berlin, Beijing and Zürich. The

A310 was returned in January 1995, but leased again, together with one other, from Airbus Industrie Financial Services for five years in May 1998.

Air Malta operated a wet-leased 221-seat A310-300, its first wide-body aircraft, from Sabena between December 1994 and December 1995. Air Europe Italy used several aircraft on wet-lease from Oasis, flying holiday charters out of Milan Malpensa. Now defunct Turkish charter carrier Holiday Airlines operated an A310-203 on lease from Airbus between 23 June and 12 October 1994. Air Plus Comet started operations on 1 March 1997 with a charter flight from Madrid to Varadero in Cuba. It operates three leased 265-seat A310-300s, which were delivered in March and May 1997 and January 1999, on charter services to Aruba, Cancun, Cartagena, Margarita Island, Miami, New York and Varadero.

RIGHT: Sakha Airlines A310-300.

BELOW RIGHT: Jes Air A310-222. *R Wallner*

BELOW: Trans European Airways (TEA) A310-300.

FAR EASTERN FORAY

The A310 lost out to the larger capacity A300 in the Far East, but could still be seen in several countries, albeit in small numbers and mainly for short periods only. Indonesian carrier Merpati Nusantara operated two leased A310-300s on domestic and regional services, putting the type on to the Jakarta–Ujung Pandang–Manado route at the end of August 1996. They were also scheduled to Denpasar/Bali, which served as an intermediate stop on the routes to Perth and Melbourne in Australia, carrying principally tourist traffic. The last service was flown on 27 June 1998. Neighbouring Malaysia Airlines leased a Royal Jordanian A310-300 between 1 March and 1 November 1990, while start-up Adorna Airways operated an A310-300 leased from Aerocancun during a short-lived existence from April 1997.

The Brunei Government took delivery of a new A310-300 on 12 June 1987 for use by the Sultan's Flight as a VIP transport. Royal Nepal Airlines supplemented its Boeing 757s for a time with a single A310-300, leased from Polaris leasing between 10 December 1993 and May 1996. Vietnam Airlines sub-leased an ex-China Eastern A310-200 in 1992 from Bulgarian carrier Jes-Air, and an ex-TAP Air Portugal A310-300 from Singapore's Regionair between 1 December 1992 and 4 January 1994. Regionair had itself leased the aircraft from GATX.

The Mongolian flag-carrier Mongolian Airlines signed an agreement with Airbus Industrie Financial Services on 28 April 1998 for an A310-300, becoming a new Airbus customer. The ex-Lufthansa A310-300, powered by the CF6-80C2 turbofan engine, is configured to carry 169 passengers, with 12 in first, 40 in business and 117 in economy classes. It entered service on 9 June 1998 and serves the airline's premium routes from Ulan Bator to Moscow, Berlin, Beijing, Seoul and Osaka.

ABOVE: Merpati Nusantara A310-300.

LEFT: Mongolian Airlines A310-300.

BELOW: Royal Nepal A310-300. *Neil Clarke*

FedEx

The world's largest transportation company Federal Express (FedEx) includes among its nearly 600-strong fleet a total of 39 A310-200F freighters, all converted from passenger configuration between 1994 and 1998. The first aircraft, one of 13 ex-Lufthansa machines, was delivered in June 1994, with the last arriving at Memphis in January 1998. The fleet also includes 12 ex-KLM aircraft, three from Swissair, two from Sabena, two previously leased by Air Liberté, and seven from Delta Air Lines. The A310-200F can carry up to 40 tonnes of cargo.

Hapag Lloyd

One of Germany's principal charter airlines, Hapag Lloyd took delivery of four A310-200s during 1988, the first arriving at Hanover on 1 February in time for the summer holiday season. A requirement for greater range resulted in further orders, with three A310-300s joining the fleet, one each in 1989, 1990 and 1992. A fourth was operated on lease from GECAS between 20 March 1995 and June 1998. The seven A310s fly the airline's long-haul inclusive-tour services to North and Central America, the Caribbean, and on the longer routes to the Mediterranean Basin, fitted out for 264 passengers.

ABOVE: Federal Express (FedEx) A310-200F.

ABOVE RIGHT: Hapag Lloyd A310-200.

RIGHT: Iberworld A310-300.

IBERWORLD

Spanish newcomer Iberworld Airlines has been leasing an A310-300 from Translux Airlines since February 1999, to add medium- to long-haul charter routes to its portfolio of services. The first A310 service was flown on 25 February between Tenerife and Helsinki, but the aircraft primarily operates services to Cancun, Punta Cana and Puerto Plata in Central America.

INTERFLUG

On 7 June 1988, the East German airline Interflug became the first Airbus customer from the Soviet Bloc, signing a contract for three A310-300s, powered by General Electric turbofan engines. The contract was part of a plan to modernise the Soviet fleet with new western aircraft. The first two arrived in June 1989, but by the time the third was delivered on 23 October 1989, the two Germanys had been re-united, precipitating the collapse of the Communist system. The A310s replaced Ilyushin IL-62Ms on routes from Berlin/Schönefeld to such points as Beijing, Havana, Moscow and Singapore. Interflug ceased operations in 1991 and the three A310s were bought by the Luftwaffe on 1 May that same year.

RIGHT: Kenya Airways A310-300 in previous markings.

BOTTOM RIGHT: KLM Royal Dutch Airlines A310-200.

BELOW: Interflug A310-300.

KENYA AIRWAYS

A rare order from Africa came Airbus' way on 8 October 1985, when the Kenyan flag-carrier signed a contract for two A310-300s, becoming the first customer for the A310 on that continent. Prior to the delivery of the new aircraft on 15 May and 24 September 1986, Kenya Airways had leased a Condor aircraft between 26 October 1985 and 22 May 1986. The new aircraft were put onto routes within Africa, and to Europe and the Indian subcontinent. A third aircraft was acquired on lease from ILFC on 28 November 1989. The three aircraft were initially fitted out with 12 first-class sleeperettes, 39 business-class and 144 economy-class seats, but are now operated in a two-class layout for 205 passengers in an 18 business/187 economy split, as is a fourth aircraft acquired on lease in March 1999. Among destinations served are Copenhagen, Dubai, Frankfurt, Jeddah, Karachi, Mumbai, Paris, Rome, Stockholm and Zürich.

KLM ROYAL DUTCH AIRLINES

KLM became the fourth A310 customer in a two-week order spree led off by Swissair, placing the biggest ever single aircraft order in its history for 10 A310-200s, plus 10 options, on 3 April 1979. Although the first aircraft was officially delivered on 26 April 1983, disagreements between management and staff delayed service entry for a few weeks. Fitted out initially for 215 passengers, later reduced to 206 seats, the A310s were progressively introduced onto the routes to London, Istanbul, Madrid, Milan, Athens and Cairo, with other Middle Eastern

and North African destinations added later. The tenth and last A310 was delivered on 25 September 1985. As part of a general move towards Boeing aircraft, the Dutch flag-carrier started to phase out its A310s from October 1995, in a lease-exchange deal with ILFC for the Boeing 767. Most of the A310s went on to serve with FedEx.

KUWAIT AIRWAYS
The order for six A310-200s, placed on 27 June 1980, marked a significant breakthrough for Airbus, as Kuwait Airways' fleet

was then entirely made up of Boeing aircraft. Three months later, a further two were ordered, plus three of the new A300-600C. Kuwait Airways took delivery of its first aircraft on 28 September 1983 and placed the type into service in November on routes to Abu Dhabi, Algiers, Amsterdam, London and Tripoli. The last three of the eight aircraft, delivered in 1984, were not required and were immediately sold to Boeing! Kuwait Airways suffered badly during the conflict with Iraq, when the five A310s in service were seized on 2 August 1990. Although they returned to Kuwait in September 1991, the airline was

already leasing five A310-300s from Polaris Leasing in the aftermath of the Gulf War, and the original five were sold to Airbus in November 1992. The Polaris aircraft also left the fleet soon after, being replaced by four new A310-300s, delivered between 19 May and 2 November 1993. One of these is operated for the Kuwaiti Government.

LAB Airlines

The A310 has served the main routes of Lloyd Aereo Boliviano (LAB), the Bolivian flag-carrier, since leasing an A310-300 from Royal Jordanian between 16 June and 15 August 1991. This was followed on 20 November that same year by another on lease from ILFC, which remains in service alongside a second aircraft, also leased from the same source and delivered on 27 September 1996. Yet another A310-300 was leased for a time from 18 May 1995. The two aircraft, fitted out with 18 business and 191 economy class seats, fly the airline's services from Santa Cruz de la Sierra to La Paz, Buenos Aires, Manaus, Montevideo and Miami.

LEFT: Kuwait Airways A310-300

BELOW: LAB Airlines (Lloyd Aereo Boliviano) A310-300

LATIN LICENCE

Aerocancun, a newly-formed Mexican associate of the Spanish Oasis International Group, took delivery of an A310-300 on 13 December 1991 and put the type into service on its charter routes within the Americas, and across the Atlantic to Europe.

The A310 spent a short lease with Air Ambar, a charter airline based at Santo Domingo in the Dominican Republic, which operated the aircraft on flights between Europe and Central America from October 1995 to November 1996. From 31 December 1996 and 31 October 1997 it flew with Dinar Lineas Aereas on charters from Buenos Aires to the Caribbean. Aerocancun itself leased others for short periods from Oasis, but ceased operations in early 1999.

Antiguan-registered Caribjet, essentially a wet-lease specialist, acquired two ex-Delta A310-300s on 20 December 1994 and 9 January 1995, and leased both immediately to Air-India, which also operated two wet-leased A310-300s from Canadian company Air Club International. Passaredo Transportes Aereas, a Brazilian bus company which has developed a growing airline business, is operating two A310-300s on charter services to the northeastern summer resorts of Recife, Natal and Fortaleza, as well as to the Caribbean. Operated in an all-economy layout for 247 passengers, the aircraft were delivered in December 1997 and June 1998 and are ex-Sabena and Aerocancun respectively.

Both major Ecuadorean carriers, Ecuatoreana de Aviacion and SAETA Air Ecuador, opted for the A310 in the early 1990s, but had mixed fortunes. National carrier Ecuatoriana took advantage of Pan Am's demise to acquire early delivery positions for two A310-300s, which arrived at Quito in September 1991. But the airline's financial health deteriorated and operations ceased in early 1993. Both aircraft were repossessed in March and leased to Uzbekistan Airways. Ecuatoriana's US routes had by then already been re-assigned to SAETA, which began a four-times a week service to New York in May 1992, using a brand-new A310-300 leased from ILFC. SAETA also leased another from ILFC on 22 January 1993, but this was returned on 27 September 1996. Ecuatoriana has since been resurrected and operates a single A310-300 on wet-lease from its majority Brazilian owner VASP, which had been one of the first customers for the A310 with an order for four, which were never delivered.

RIGHT: Passaredo T.A. A310-300.

BELOW RIGHT: SAETA Air Ecuador A310-300.

BELOW: Aerocancun A310-300.

LUFTHANSA

Since the German flag-carrier had been the principal driving force behind the development of the A310, the massive order on 2 April 1979 for up to 50 of the new type came as no surprise. The order for 25 aircraft, plus an equal number of options included the conversion of nine A300 options to the A310. Delivery of the first A310-200 took place on 29 March 1983 and the type went into service on 10 April, flying a Frankfurt–Stuttgart sector in the morning, followed later that day with a trip to London.

A total of eight were delivered in 1983, three in 1985 for service with charter subsidiary Condor, and two in 1986. All 13 were converted to cargo and delivered to Federal Express between July 1994 and July 1995. The remaining 12 of the original order, including two for Condor, were delivered as A310-300s between April 1987 and February 1992. Four remain in service with Lufthansa on short and medium-haul routes within Germany, Europe, Africa and the Middle East, four having been sold to the Luftwaffe (German Air Force), while two more are being leased to Luxembourg-based newcomer Solid'Air.

MARTINAIR

The Dutch charter airline placed an order for three A310-200s on 30 October 1979 and took out an option on one more. The first aircraft, in an all-passenger layout, was delivered on 15 March 1984 and took over holiday flights to the Mediterranean resorts in the summer, while being used on worldwide ad-hoc charters in the winter. On 29 November that same year, Martinair took delivery of a convertible A310-200C, configured for 256 passengers in a single-class cabin, or for up to 38 tonnes of freight. The second A310-200C on order was never taken up. Both eventually found their way to KLM, which operated them for a short time before their sale to FedEx.

MIDDLE EAST AIRLINES

The Lebanese airline began its search for a wide-body twin in 1979 and made public in November 1980 its intention to order five A310s and take options on another 14 aircraft. The airline was keen to become the launch customer for the Rolls-Royce RB211-524, but eventually settled for the Pratt & Whitney JT9D, when the UK engine failed to promise sufficient fuel burn advantage. Although MEA inked in the contract on 30 October 1981, the continued attacks on Beirut Airport during the increasingly bitter civil war, resulting in loss of traffic and operational difficulties, plunged the airline into the red and put the order into jeopardy. Eventually, it was cancelled altogether, but it was not the end. MEA started leasing three A310-200s from Lufthansa and two A310-300s from KLM, for one-year periods in 1992 and 1993, before taking two A310-300s on long-term lease from Polaris on 3 September 1993 and 10 June 1994. These were joined by three ex-Singapore Airlines A310-200s between July 1997 and March 1998, and the five aircraft now fly MEA's routes from Beirut to its principal destinations in Europe.

ABOVE: Lufthansa A310-300.

ABOVE RIGHT: Martinair A310-200C.

RIGHT: Middle East Airlines (MEA) A310-200.

MIX AND MATCH

Cameroon Airlines wet-leased an A310-300 from Air Plus Comet in November 1997. It had planned to use it throughout the winter season until the following March, but returned the aircraft on 5 December. On the other side of the African continent, a restructured Air Djibouti began operations with a leased A310-200 on 25 July 1998, serving its main links between Djibouti and Addis Ababa, Cairo, Dar-es-Salaam, Dubai, Jeddah, Johannesburg, Karachi, Khartoum, Mogadishu, Mombasa, Muscat, Nairobi and Rome. The aircraft was returned to Airbus Industrie Financial Services in February 1999.

Egyptian start-up Heliopolis Airlines operated an A310-200 from Airbus Industrie Financial Services in October 1997, but a fall-off in tourist traffic hit the airline hard and the Airbus was repossessed on 30 June 1998. Tunis Air, already an A300 operator, leased an A310-300 from Royal Jordanian between 30 August and 30 September 1991.

Qatar Airways, formed in direct competition with its own national airline Gulf Air, began operations on 20 January 1994, initially using a single ex-Kuwait Airways Pratt & Whitney-powered A310-200 leased from the manufacturer. A second ex-Kuwait Airways model followed in June 1994. A network was established linking Qatar's capital Doha with London and several destinations in East Africa and the Indian subcontinent. As services grew, the airline needed larger aircraft and the A310s were returned in February and May 1995. Another local carrier Oman Air has revamped its operations with two ex-Swissair A310-300s, which entered service in April 1999 on longer sectors from Muscat to the Indian sub-continent. New services to southern Europe and East Africa are being planned.

Luxembourg-based newcomer Solid'air was due to begin operations in spring 1999 with two A310-300s, configured for 232 passengers in a two-class cabin of 28 business and 204 economy seats. Both aircraft are being leased from Lufthansa for a period of five years for planned charter services from Luxembourg to Orlando and Fort Lauderdale in Florida, and to the Bahamas and Dominican Republic. Other Central American and Caribbean destinations will be added.

RIGHT: Air Djibouti A310-200. *Carsten Jørgensen*

BELOW RIGHT: Heliopolis Airlines A310-200. *Pedro Fernandes*

BELOW: Qatar Airways A310-300.

NIGERIA AIRWAYS

The Nigerian flag-carrier became the 40th Airbus customer, and only the second in Africa, when it placed an order for four A310-200s on 17 April 1980, for deliveries starting at the end of 1983. Options were also taken out for four more, but these were never taken up. The new aircraft were required to cope with domestic and regional expansion, and to initiate a fleet modernisation programme, but financial reasons forced a delay. All four finally joined the fleet on 14 December 1984. They were used on the airline's main service to London, as well as some regional routes in West Africa, but suffered from the airline's precarious financial and operational position, with most of the fleet unserviceable at some time. Only one is now in operation.

OASIS INTERNATIONAL AIRLINES

The Spanish charter carrier Oasis International placed an order with Airbus for four A310-300s on 9 September 1989, taking delivery of the first aircraft on 13 December 1991. This was immediately leased to Mexican sister company Aerocancun, but Oasis accepted the second in its own colours on 15 April 1992, and subsequently leased another from Airbus on 8 June 1995, and three more from Polaris/GECAS in summer 1996. However, the airline's financial situation deteriorated dramatically and most were returned to the lessors before it entered into bankruptcy proceedings in December 1996. The last A310 was impounded at New York on 15 December after operating the last flight.

PAKISTAN INTERNATIONAL AIRLINES

Already a prolific A300 operator, the Pakistani flag-carrier signed a contract on 8 August 1989 for three A310-300s, to be powered by the General Electric CF6-80C2A8 turbofan. Options were also taken out for three more, which were subsequently converted to firm orders. The smaller A310 was put on some of the airline's regional routes, following delivery of the three aircraft in summer 1991. The second batch of three joined the fleet one a year in 1992, 1993 and 1994. They are fitted out with 12 club class and 169 economy class seats and fly services to Amman, Beijing, Dhaka, Singapore, Tokyo, and on thinner European routes.

PAN AMERICAN

Having successfully operated the A300, Pan American World Airways provided a further boost to Airbus on 24 May 1985, when it placed a massive US$1.5 billion order for 12 A310-300s, including 13 options, plus 16 A320s and 34 options. Pending delivery of the A310-300s, Pan Am also ordered four A310-200s which were available for immediate delivery from a cancelled VASP order. Pan Am also acquired three ex-Kuwait Airways A310-200s in February 1986, before taking delivery of

LEFT: Nigeria Airways A310-200. *Carsten Jørgensen*

BELOW LEFT: Oasis International Airlines A310-300.

BELOW: Pakistan International Airlines A310-300.

the first two of 14 A310-300s on 17 June 1987. The A310s were used primarily in the Americas, although some flights were operated across the Atlantic, until the declining fortunes of the airline resulted in bankruptcy in December 1991. All 21 A310s were taken over by Delta Air Lines.

ROYAL AVIATION

This growing Canadian scheduled and charter operator acquired four A310-300s, primarily to provide additional capacity to fulfil its agreement with Nouvelles Frontiers. It took three on lease from Airbus and GECAS during 1997, the aircraft arriving at the airline's Montreal base in April, May and June. The fourth, an ex-Lufthansa machine completed the fleet on 25 May 1998. The A310s serve mainly holiday destinations in North America, Mexico and the Caribbean.

ROYAL JORDANIAN

The national airline of the Hashemite Kingdom of Jordan began the re-equipment and modernisation of its fleet by ordering six A310-300s and six A320s on 9 May 1986. The first two aircraft arrived in Amman in spring 1987, with the sixth and final A310 joining the fleet on 16 March 1990. The

BELOW: Pan American A310-200.

RIGHT: Royal Aviation A310-300.

BELOW RIGHT: Royal Jordanian A310-300.

two early models were sold to the French L'Armée de L'Air on 5 November 1993. The six A310s, including two A310-200s on long-term lease from Air Algérie, can be seen at several regional and European airports including those to Ankara, Beirut, Casablanca, Damascus, Delhi, Frankfurt, Istanbul, London, Madrid, Rome and Vienna.

SABENA

The Belgian airline was among the last of the European flag-carriers to join the Airbus camp, but finally signed up for three Pratt & Whitney-powered A310-200s on 31 October 1979, at the same time taking options on a further three, although these were not taken up. With the airline's poor financial health, the government questioned the need for the A310 and it was not until the setting up of a special leasing company that finance was secured for the acquisition of the aircraft. Delivery of two aircraft was accomplished on 23 February and 30 March 1984. The third followed on 3 March 1987, and a fourth was leased from Airbus on 20 December 1994, but was immediately sub-leased to Air Malta. Following the acquisition of a major stake in the airline by Swissair and subsequent restructuring, the A310 operated its last service on 2 September 1997, the remaining three aircraft all joining the FedEx fleet.

SINGAPORE AIRLINES

Already an A300 operator, the Singapore flag-carrier found that aircraft too large for its Far Eastern regional routes and ordered six A310-200s with Pratt & Whitney JTD9 engines on 31 May 1983. The six aircraft were delivered between 19 November 1984 and 30 April 1994 and took over the routes to Bangkok, Hong Kong, Jakarta, Kuala Lumpur, Manila, Penang, Seoul and Taipei. The A310 became an immediate success and Singapore Airlines added another 17, this time the

ABOVE: Singapore Airlines A310-300.

BELOW: Sabena A310-200.

RIGHT: Somali Airlines A310-300.

longer-range A310-300 with PW4152 engines, between 1987 and 1995, fitted out for 183 passengers in a three-class layout. Four of the earlier –200 models were leased to regional subsidiary SilkAir from 1993 to 1995, before the disposal of all six during 1997. One went to the Belgian Air Force on 25 September 1997, while the others will be converted to cargo for FedEx.

SOMALI AIRLINES

The now defunct national carrier Somali Airlines announced an order for one A310-300 and one option on 15 October 1987, becoming a new Airbus customer. The General-Electric-powered A310 was to be delivered in October 1988 but a delay forced the airline to lease a Sabena A310-200 for a few months, taking delivery on 17 October 1988. This aircraft was returned to Belgium on arrival of the new aircraft on 20 March 1989. Configured with 14 seats in first class, in business and 147 in economy, the A310 was used on non-stop routes from the airline's home base at Mogadishu to cities in Europe and the Middle East. The deteriorating political situation in the country resulted in the suspension of services and the Airbus was repossessed on 1 January 1991.

LEFT: Sudan Airways A310-300.

BELOW LEFT: Swissair A310-300.

BELOW: Balair A310-300.

SUDAN AIRWAYS

The A310-300 had been the flagship of the Sudan Airways fleet since leasing its first from Royal Jordanian between 1 December 1990 and 1 April 1991. A year later, it leased two further aircraft, with the last returned to its lessor in April 1996. Next came an A310-200s leased from Airbus Industrie Financial Services in May 1997, replaced by a similar model on 28 July 1997. This too has now been returned. While in service with Sudan Airways, the A310s flew the main routes from Khartoum to Abu Dhabi, Amman, Doha, Dubai, Jeddah, London, Moroni, N'djamena, Paris, Riyadh and Sharjah.

SWISSAIR

As joint launch customer with Lufthansa, Swissair became the first airline to place an order for the new A310 when it signed up for 10, plus 10 options, on 15 March 1979. The airline took delivery of its first Pratt & Whitney-powered A310-200 on 25 March 1983 and operated its first revenue flight on 21 April. Four aircraft were delivered in 1983, one in 1984, two in 1985 and the final three in 1986, including one for charter subsidiary Balair. Four of these were of the extended range version for use on Middle Eastern and West African routes. The first five aircraft were sold to International Lease Finance Corporation (ILFC) on 15 March 1994 and leased back for one year before going into service with Federal Express. The remaining five aircraft, all A310-300s, were due to be phased out by the end of

1999. Subsidiary BalairCTA operates three extended-range A310-300s, acquired new in April 1992 and May 1995.

TAP AIR PORTUGAL

The A310 was the first Airbus in the fleet of the Portuguese national airline. An initial contract for two A310-300s, placed on 22 February 1988, was quickly followed by further orders, bringing the fleet to six aircraft with the final delivery on 7 May 1991. The last aircraft, however, was directly sold to GATX and leased back until 30 September 1992. The first aircraft had been delivered on 25 October 1988. The five aircraft are now scheduled from Lisbon to such destinations as Abidjan, Amsterdam, Brazzaville, Dakar, Frankfurt, London, Ponta Delgada, Sao Tomé and Terceira.

TAROM ROMANIAN AIR TRANSPORT

Following the general trend for East European airlines to graduate to modern Western equipment, Romania's flag-carrier ordered two A310-300s, which both arrived at Bucharest on 17 December 1992. The first flight with the new type was operated on Christmas Eve over the Bucharest–Paris route. A third aircraft, previously operated by Pan American and Delta Air Lines, was acquired on 11 April 1994 but crashed shortly after take-off from Bucharest on 31 March the following year. Typical destinations served with the two A310s are Chicago, New York, Brussels, Paris, Larnaca, Tel Aviv, Abu Dhabi, Dubai, Delhi and Beijing.

THAI AIRWAYS INTERNATIONAL

Thailand's domestic carrier Thai Airways ordered two A310-200s on 29 March 1985 to provide more capacity on its main trunk routes linking Bangkok with Chiang Mai in the North, and Phuket and Hat Yai in the South. It took delivery of its two aircraft, both with the newly-introduced wing tip fences, on 29 April and 26 November 1986, but both were transferred to Thai Airways International on 1 April 1988 when domestic and international operations were merged into a single carrier. One aircraft remains in service, the other having perished on approach to Surat Thani in poor weather on 11 December 1998. Thai International also leased two ex-Canadian Airlines A310-300s in May 1990, one of which unfortunately crashed near Kathmandu, Nepal on 31 July 1992. The other was returned to the lessor on 31 August 1993.

TRANSAVIA

After leasing an A300B2 during 1976, Transavia re-established its Airbus association 22 years later with the lease of a Pratt & Whitney PW4152-powered A310-324. The aircraft was leased from Translux International Airlines on 6 May 1998 for a four-

RIGHT: Tarom Romanian Airlines A310-300.

BELOW RIGHT: Thai Airways International A310-200.

BELOW: TAP Air Portugal A310-300.

month period, entering service on a charter between Amsterdam and Malaga. Typical charter destinations served included Alicante, Corfu, Fuerteventura, Heraklion, Malaga, Malta, Rhodes and Tenerife.

TURKISH AIRLINES

The Turkish flag-carrier became a new Airbus customer on 7 December 1984, signing up for seven General-Electric-powered A310-200s for early delivery, at the same time taking out seven more options. Four arrived in Istanbul in 1985, starting on 22 May, and three in 1986. Turkish Airlines quickly took up its options, taking delivery of seven longer-range A310-300s between 11 April 1988 and 11 July 1991. All 14 remain in service, flying on some of the main routes from Istanbul to destinations in Europe and the Middle East. Several other A310s were leased from Lufthansa for short periods during 1993.

UZBEKISTAN AIRWAYS

The flag-carrier of the newly-independent state of Uzbekistan began operating two second-hand A310-300s on lease from June 1993 on its international network to Western Europe and Eastern Asia. It added a third, purchased direct from the manu-

LEFT: Turkish Airlines A310-300.

BELOW LEFT: Uzbekistan Airways A310-300.

BELOW: Wardair Canada A310-300.

facturer, on 15 June 1998, all fitted out comfortably for 192 passengers, comprising 12 first-class, 30 business-class and 150 economy-class seats. The A310s fly on average 12 hours 30 minutes each day on routes from Tashkent to such cities as Amsterdam, Bangkok, Beijing, Frankfurt, Jakarta, Kuala Lumpur, Malé, London, New York and Tel Aviv.

WARDAIR CANADA

The Canadian charter airline became the first in North America to order the A310, signing a purchase agreement with Airbus for six A310-200s on 25 March 1981. Although deliveries were requested to start in November 1983, a slump in traffic forced a postponement and the first aircraft was not delivered until 25 November 1987. However, the situation had improved dramatically by that time, and the airline took delivery of two more in 1987, followed by nine in 1988. All were A310-300s, rather than the -200s first ordered. Two further orders remained unfulfilled, as a result of Wardair being acquired and merged into Canadian Airlines International on 16 October 1989. The 12 A310s, used on domestic, Caribbean and Central American charters, passed to the new owner, but the aircraft did not fit into its operational structure and all were sold to leasing companies in 1990 and 1991. Five found their way to the Canadian Armed Forces at the beginning of 1993.

YEMENIA

Yemenia-Yemen Airways Corporation began A310 operations on 14 April 1995, when it leased two A310-200s from Airbus for its services linking Aden and Sana'a with Abu Dhabi, Dubai, Mumbai, Sharjah and London. On 31 December that year, the national airline placed an order for two new A310-300s, which replaced the earlier models in March 1997 and includes the last A310 built to date. The new A310s are configured in a two-class layout with 190 seats. Prior to its merger with Yemenia, Aden-based Alyemda had operated a single leased A310-300 between June 1993 and June 1996.

BELOW: Yemenia A310-300.

BOTTOM: Alyemda A310-300.

ABOVE: Costa Rican carrier LACSA ordered two A310-300s, but never took delivery.

BELOW: Iraqi Airways ordered the A310, but the aircraft were never delivered because the Gulf War intervened.

6 ACCIDENTS AND INCIDENTS

It would be against the laws of probability, if the A310 had not suffered any losses in 15 years of service. Yet, there have been only four accidents among the 261 aircraft built to date, none of which could be traced to any technical malfunction of the airframe or systems. While the manufacturer can make use of the latest technology to produce as safe an aircraft as is possible, he can do little about human fallibility, and in one case stupidity, nor about severe weather complications. Both elements, either separately or in conjunction, have had a hand in the four crashes.

RUSSIAN ROULETTE

The crash of A310-308 F-GOQS of Aeroflot Russian International Airlines, the first of a western aircraft in service with a Russian airline, drew a considerable amount of publicity, especially after the findings of the accident enquiry. What eventually emerged after extensive probing by the media, was that the Aeroflot captain had handed control of the aircraft over to his 16-year old son.

Flight SU593 had left Moscow's Sheremetyevo Airport on 22 March 1994, on a regular scheduled flight to Hong Kong, carrying 63 passengers, mostly Russians, and 12 crew. About four hours into the 10 hour flight, the aircraft descended rapidly from its 30,000 ft (9,150 m) cruising altitude and crashed in the remote mountain region of Kemeroskoi, in the Altay Mountains near the town of Mezhdurechensk in Western Siberia. It was dark at the time, and the last transmission from the aircraft some 15 minutes before impact provided no indication of any problems. Two Antonov An-12s were dispatched and two helicopters located the burnt-out wreckage at dawn. Rescue attempts were hampered by thick snow, but none of the 75 people on board survived the then puzzling accident.

The initial draft of the accident report indicated that the crash had been the result of "unfavourable occurrence of a number of factors, such as the presence of children in the cockpit, the crew's insufficient knowledge of operational procedures of flying a foreign aircraft, as well as a series of other circumstances". These words, however, glossed over what essentially amounted to a complete disregard by the flight crew of the rules of safe flight deck procedure. Details of the report by the Russian Aviation Committee (MAK), which appeared in an official newspaper, stated that Capt Yaroslav Kudrinsky's 12-year old daughter and 16-year old son Eldar occupied his seat at various times. There was also a third pilot in the cockpit, who had travelled on the flight as a passenger. Excerpts from the transcript leading up to the crash, as published in *Flight International*, reads as follows:

Eldar: Can I turn this?
Captain: What?

Eldar: The wheel?
Captain: Yes. If you turn it left, where will the plane go?
Eldar: Left.
Captain: Turn it! Watch the ground as you turn. Let's go left. Is the plane turning?
Eldar: Great!
Captain: Is it turning? Is the plane turning left?
Eldar: Yes, it is.
One of the pilots: Set the horizon right for him.

(Conversation between Captain and daughter)

Eldar: Why is it turning?
Captain: It's turning by itself?
Eldar: Yes!
Unidentified co-pilot: Hey guys!
Captain: Hold on, hold the wheel, hold it. To the left! To the left! To the right!
Co-pilot: To the other side!
Eldar: I am turning it left!

The pilot then tells his son to " . . . crawl back! Get away", repeating the instruction 12 times. It appears that the boy was unable to move because of the g force caused by the steeply turning aircraft. According to *Flight*, he then pushed the right rudder pedal as the pilot tried to free him, putting the Airbus into a spin. Although the pilot was able to arrest the spin, the aircraft was too low to prevent the crash.

PULL UP . . . PULL UP . . .

The first A310 came to grief on a mountainside on approach to Kathmandu in Nepal. Thai Airways International Flight TG311, an A310-304 registered HS-TID, was conducting the Sierra VOR/DME approach to runway 02 at Tribhuvan International Airport on 31 July 1992, when a flap fault (later rectified by retracting and reselecting the flaps) caused the crew to ask for clearance back to Calcutta. The crew decided that it was not possible to continue the straight-in approach, due to the steep descent angles required and the position of the aircraft, and requested a turn back to the Romeo fix. There ensued several discussions with the controller during which it was determined that the aircraft was to maintain an altitude of 11,500ft and was "to proceed to Romeo". The cockpit voice recorder showed that the crew was in the process of inserting navigational information into the flight management system (FMS), but was experiencing difficulties. The flight was continuing north, instead of towards the Romeo point to the south, when the ground proximity warning system (GPWS) sounded the warning "terrain, terrain", followed by "whoop, whoop, pull-up". The aural warning continued until impact 16 seconds later at the 11.500ft level of a 16,000ft high Himalayan peak. All 99 passengers and 14 crew members lost their lives.

The report findings highlighted 57 points, but the probable causes were given as ineffective communication between the area control centre and the flight crew, which allowed the flight to proceed in the wrong direction; failure to transmit the aircraft's position; and ineffective crew co-ordination of flight navigational duties. Contributing factors were given as the misleading depiction of Romeo on the operator's approach chart used by the crew, the flap fault which required the initial approach to be discontinued, and inadequate radio communication that stemmed from language difficulties and failed to resolve problems.

Thai International lost a second A310 on 11 December 1998, when flight TG261 plunged into a flooded rubber plantation less than a mile from the Surat Thani airport terminal after attempting a third landing in heavy rain and cloud. The A310-204 HS-TIA left Bangkok for Surat Thani in the southwest of Thailand in the afternoon, carrying 132 passengers and 14 crew. It was flown by experienced ex-Royal Thai Air Force Captain Pinit Wechasilpa, who, along with his first officer and 100 passengers and cabin crew, died in the crash. The pilots were attempting to land in heavy rain and low clouds, but decided to go around. On the second attempt, the captain maintained the approach heading and flew over the terminal before turning 190°, as prescribed for a missed-approach procedure. On the third attempt, the aircraft pitched up sharply and entered a steep climb before crashing to the ground. The crew was performing a VOR/DME approach, as the instrument landing system (ILS) had been removed during runway extension work, and there were suggestions that some of the runway lights were not working. The report had not been issued at the time of writing.

SNOWSTORM
On 31 March 1995, at 0810 local time, Tarom A310-324 YR-LCC crashed in a heavy snowstorm and sleet two minutes after take-off from Bucharest en route to Brussels, killing 49 passengers and 11 crew. At the time, there were reports of an explosion at the back of the aircraft, and the airline revealed that it

had received bomb threats for some weeks prior to the accident, but there was no positive evidence of sabotage. Indeed, the primary cause, as outlined in the official report, appears to have been a mechanically jammed throttle lever in the full power position (due to unidentified reasons), while the autothrottle was engaged. The report by the Romanian Accident Investigation Committee suggested the pilots did nothing in rectifying the resultant asymmetric thrust, which took more than 40 seconds to develop, until just before impact. The pilot had begun a 25° bank left turn as required by procedures, but the increasing power asymmetry, said the report, caused the aircraft's 18° nose-up pitch to decrease to zero, and the bank to increase," . . . as the aircraft continued to roll over laterally to more than 170° to the left, while the pitch seems to have reached 80° nose-down." According to the report, only small rudder and elevator deflections were recorded throughout, and that engine number two was reduced to idle a few seconds before the end of the recording.

The Romanian airline had suffered two other incidents with another A310, but thankfully neither ended in tragedy. On 24 September 1994, during its final approach to Paris Orly when the Airbus was flying at 2,500ft (760m), the aircraft went into a 'level-change' mode (altitude-control normally set manually), causing the autothrottle levers to move forward and resulting in an increase in thrust and corresponding increase in pitch. Various manoeuvres with the control column while the autothrottle was left connected, resulted in further increase in pitch and roll to the left. At that point the autothrottle disconnected and the pilot was able to regain control and landed normally. The same aircraft was flying from Chicago to Amsterdam on 1 March 1995, when it suddenly entered into a 30° nose-up, 12,000ft/minute climb to 40,500ft, before plunging through its assigned flight level and levelling out. No-one was hurt and the flight continued to its destination without further incident.

CASUALTY RECORD
The following table summaries the four accidents, which have resulted in write-off of the aircraft up to September 1999. This includes one A310-200 and three A310-300 variants.

C/n	Registration	Operator	Model	Date	Location	Type of accident
415	HS-TIA	Thai Airways International	-204	11/12/98	Surat Thani	Crashed on approach in poor weather, 101 killed
438	HS-TID	Thai Airways International	-304	31/07/92	nr Kathmandu	Crashed into mountain, 111 killed
450	YR-LCC	Tarom	-324	31/03/95	Bucharest	Crashed on take-off, 60 killed
596	F-OGQS	Aeroflot	-308	23/03/94	nr Novokuznetsk	Crashed into wooded terrain close to Mezhdurechensk, 75 killed

7 PRODUCTION HISTORY

The following table provides the complete production, including the first customer delivery. Airbus test registrations, used on most aircraft, are not shown. Unless specifically indicated otherwise in the remarks column as written off (w/o), broken up (b/u) or stored (st), aircraft remains in active service. Ntu stands for orders cancelled and not taken up. Write-offs shown did not necessarily occur in the service of the original operator — for full details see separate casualty record. Names in italics are those first applied to individual aircraft by the initial operator. Airbus built a total of 261 aircraft over a 15-year period, including 85 of the -200 variant and 176 -300s.

C/N	Reg'n	Owner/operator	Model	First Flight	Delivery	Remarks
162	HB-IPE	Swissair	-221	03/04/82	21/03/84	*Basel-Land*
172	F-GEMF	Air France	-203	13/05/82	14/03/86	
191	D-AICA	Lufthansa	-203	05/08/82	09/03/84	*Neustadt an der Weinstrasse*
201	D-AICB	Lufthansa	-203	20/10/82	29/03/83	*Garmish Partenkirchen*
217	HB-IPC	Swissair	-221	01/12/82	28/06/83	*Schwyz*
224	HB-IPA	Swissair	-221	05/01/83	25/03/83	*Aargau*
230	D-AICC	Lufthansa	-203	27/01/83	27/03/83	*Kaiserslautern*
233	D-AICD	Lufthansa	-203	07/02/83	27/03/83	*Detmold*
237	D-AICF	Lufthansa	-203	22/02/83	31/03/83	*Rüdesheim am Rhein*
241	PH-AGA	KLM	-203	08/03/83	26/04/83	*Rembrandt*
245	PH-AGB	KLM	-203	04/05/83	17/06/83	*Jeroen Bosch*
248	PH-AGC	KLM	-203	12/04/83	27/05/83	*Albert Cuyp*
251	HB-IPB	Swissair	-221	20/04/83	30/05/83	*Neuchatel*
254	D-AICH	Lufthansa	-203	27/04/83	01/06/83	*Lüneburg*
257	D-AICK	Lufthansa	-203	25/05/83	07/07/83	*Westerland-Sylt*
260	HB-IPD	Swissair	-221	27/06/83	14/10/83	*Solothurn*
264	PH-AGD	KLM	-203	04/08/83	12/12/83	*Marinus Ruppert*
267	9K-AHA	Kuwait Airways	-222	29/07/83	28/09/83	
270	5N-AUE	Nigeria Airways	-222	24/08/83	12/12/84	st Bordeaux
273	D-AICL	Lufthansa	-203	13/10/83	20/01/84	*Rothenburg o d Tauber*
276	9K-AHB	Kuwait Airways	-222	19/09/83	26/10/83	
278	9K-AHC	Kuwait Airways	-222	30/09/83	09/12/83	*Kadhma*
281	PH-MCA	Martinair Holland	-203	13/10/83	15/03/84	
283	PH-AGE	KLM	-203	24/10/83	13/01/84	*Jan Steen*
285	5N-AUF	Nigeria Airways	-222	09/11/83	14/12/84	*River Ethiope*, st Brussels
288	N801PA	Pan American	-221	21/11/83	25/05/85	Clipper *Berlin*,
		VASP		ntu		
291	7T-VJC	Air Algerie	-203	20/06/84	31/08/84	
293	7T-VJD	Air Algerie	-203	02/08/84	20/12/84	
295	G-BKWT	British Caledonian	-203	15/12/83	20/03/84	
297	PH-AGF	KLM	-203	21/12/83	07/02/84	*Frans Hals*
300	5B-DAQ	Cyprus Airways	-203	27/12/83	16/02/84	*Soli*
303	OO-SCA	Sabena	-222	10/01/84	23/02/84	
306	G-BKWU	British Caledonian	-203	20/01/84	20/03/84	
309	5B-DAR	Cyprus Airways	-203	03/02/84	23/03/84	
311	B-2301	CAAC	-222	29/02/84	25/06/85	MEA, ntu
313	OO-SCB	Sabena	-222	23/02/84	30/03/84	
316	F-GEMA	Air France	-203	10/03/84	27/04/84	
318	9K-AHD	Kuwait Airways	-222	16/03/84	26/04/84	*Failaka*

Aeroflot A310-300 in short-lived colours at Melbourne Tullamarine. *Günter Endres*

C/N	Reg'n	Owner/operator	Model	First Flight	Delivery	Remarks
320	B-2302	CAAC	-222	11/08/84	28/06/85	MEA, ntu
323	G-BKWV	British Caledonian	-203	order cancelled	aircraft not built	
326	F-GEMB	Air France	-203	30/03/84	04/06/84	
329	5N-AUG	Nigeria Airways	-222	02/05/84	14/12/84	*Lekki Peninsula*, st Brussels
331	9K-AHE	Kuwait Airways	-222	11/04/84	30/05/84	
333	N802PA	Pan American	-221	15/02/85	31/05/85	Clipper *Frankfurt*. VASP ntu
335	F-GEMC	Air France	-203	15/05/84	21/06/84	
338	TC-JCL	THY-Turkish Airlines	-203	05/04/85	22/05/85	*Seyhan*
339	9K-AHH	Kuwait Airways	-222	11/07/84	27/09/84	
340	5N-AUH	Nigeria Airways	-222	15/06/84	14/12/84	*Rima River*
342	9K-AHJ	Kuwait Airways	-222	28/04/84	28/09/84	
343	N803PA	Pan American	-221	27/02/85	25/05/85	Clipper *Munich*, VASP ntu
345	N804PA	Pan American	-221	21/03/85	12/06/85	Clipper *Hamburg*, VASP ntu
346	9K-AHK	Kuwait Airways	-222	20/09/84	29/10/84	
347	9V-STI	Singapore Airlines	-222	26/09/84	19/11/84	
349	PH-MCB	Martinair Holland	-203C	03/10/84	29/11/84	

C/N	Reg'n	Owner/operator	Model	First Flight	Delivery	Remarks
350	9V-STJ	Singapore Airlines	-222	15/10/84	28/11/84	
352	5B-DAS	Cyprus Airways	-203	31/01/85	28/03/85	*Salamis*
353	PH-AGG	KLM	-203	26/10/84	11/01/85	*Vincent van Gogh*
355	F-GEMD	Air France	-203	13/11/84	04/01/85	
356	D-AICM	Condor Flugdienst	-203	21/11/84	10/01/85	
357	9V-STK	Singapore Airlines	-222	27/11/84	28/01/85	
359	D-AICN	Condor Flugdienst	-203	14/12/84	07/02/85	
360	D-AICP	Condor Flugdienst	-203	26/12/84	14/02/85	
362	PH-AGH	KLM	-203	04/01/85	19/02/85	*Pieter de Hough*
363	9V-STL	Singapore Airlines	-222	17/01/85	07/03/85	
364	PH-AGI	KLM	-203	07/02/85	21/03/85	*Jan Toorop*
367	9V-STM	Singapore Airlines	-222	21/02/85	02/04/85	
369	F-GEME	Air France	-203	01/03/85	12/04/85	
370	TC-JCR	THY-Turkish Airlines	-203	06/01/86	21/02/86	*Kizilirmak*, B.Cal ntu
372	9V-STN	Singapore Airlines	-222	19/03/85	30/04/85	
373	HB-IPF	Swissair	-22`	order cancelled	not built;	replaced by c/n 399
375	TC-JCM	THY-Turkish Airlines	-203	16/04/85	30/05/85	*Ceyhan*
376	PH-AGK	KLM	-203	order cancelled	not built;	replaced by c/n 394

Diamond Sakha A310-300.

C/N	Reg'n	Owner/operator	Model	First Flight	Delivery	Remarks
378	P2-ANA	Air Niugini	-324	08/07/85	27/01/89	
379	TC-JCN	THY-Turkish Airlines	-203	24/04/85	21/06/85	*Dicle*
381			order cancelled		aircraft not built	
382			order cancelled		aircraft not built	
383			order cancelled		aircraft not built	
385			order cancelled		aircraft not built	
386	TC-JCO	THY-Turkish Airlines	-203	29/04/85	26/06/85	*Firat*
387	OE-LAA	Austrian Airlines	-221	order cancelled	not built;	replaced by c/n 499
389	TC-JCS	THY-Turkish Airlines	-203	20/01/86	12/03/86	*Yesilirmak*
390	TC-JCU	THY-Turkish Airlines	-203	19/02/86	14/04/86	*Sakarya*
392	VT-EJL	Air-India	-304	06/09/85	30/03/87	*Sabarmati*
393			order cancelled		aircraft not built	
394	PH-AGK	KLM	-203	10/07/85	25/09/85	*Johannes Vermeer*
396	OE-LAI	Austrian Airlines	-221	order cancelled	not built;	replaced by c/n 492
397	D-AICR	Lufthansa	-203	14/08/85	10/01/86	*Freudenstadt*
399	HB-IPF	Swissair	-322	16/10/85	16/12/85	*Glarus*
400	D-AICS	Lufthansa	-203	05/11/85	27/02/86	*Recklinghausen*
402			order cancelled		aircraft not built	

C/N	Reg'n	Owner/operator	Model	First Flight	Delivery	Remarks
403			order cancelled		aircraft not built	
404	HB-IPG	Swissair	-322	29/10/85	20/12/85	*Zug*
406	VT-EJG	Air-India	-304	10/02/86	11/04/86	*Yamuna*
407	VT-EJH	Air-India	-304	07/03/86	07/05/86	*Tista*
409	HB-IPH	Swissair	-322	21/11/85	15/01/86	*Appenzell i. Rh*
410	HB-IPI	Swissair	-322	29/11/85	31/01/86	*Luzern*
412	HB-IPK	Balair	-322	03/02/86	21/03/86	
413	VT-EJI	Air-India	-304	07/03/86	29/05/86	*Sarawati*
415	HS-TIA	Thai Airways	-204	03/03/86	29/04/86	w/o Surat Thani 11/12/98
416	5Y-BEL	Kenya Airways	-304	21/03/86	15/05/86	*Nyayo Star*
418	C-FSWD	Wardair Canada	-304	22/07/86	21/01/88	*A M Matt Berry*
419	B-2303	CAAC	-222	07/04/86	30/05/86	
421	F-ODVD	Royal Jordanian	-304	15/01/87	13/03/87	*Prince Hashem,*
	JY-CAD			ntu		
422	F-ODVE	Royal Jordanian	-304	03/03/87	28/04/87	*Princess Iman,*
	JY-CAE			ntu		
424	HS-TIC	Thai Airways	-204	02/06/86	26/11/86	
425	C-FWDX	Wardair Canada	-304	24/12/86	31/01/88	*H W Harry Hayter*
426	5Y-BEN	Kenya Airways	-304	03/07/86	24/09/86	*Harambee Star*
427	D-AHLW	Hapag-Lloyd	-204	19/09/86	04/01/88	
428	VT-EJJ	Air-India	-304	26/08/86	29/10/86	*Beas*
429	VT-EJK	Air-India	-304	03/09/86	29/12/86	*Gonti*
430	D-AHLV	Hapag-Lloyd	-204	25/09/86	01/02/88	
431	V8-HM1	Brunei Government	-304	11/05/87	12/06/87	
432	A6-EKA	Emirates Airline	-304	08/10/86	03/07/87	
433	9V-STO	Singapore Airlines	-324	27/04/87	08/07/87	
	PH-MCC	Martinair		ntu		
434	D-AIDA	Condor Flugdienst	-304	25/02/87	09/04/87	
435	B-2304	CAAC	-304	02/12/86	31/07/87	
436	A6-EKB	Emirates Airline	-304	02/05/87	24/07/87	
437	OO-SCC	Sabena	-322	28/11/86	03/03/87	
438	C-FGWD	Wardair Canada	-304	02/10/87	25/11/87	*Z Lewys Lee*, w/o 31/07/92
439	N811PA	Pan American	-324	21/06/87	17/07/87	Clipper *Constitution,* st Atlanta
440	B-2305	CAAC	-304	25/05/87	28/08/87	
441	C-FHWD	Wardair Canada	-304	05/10/87	28/11/87	*Don C Braun*
442	N812PA	Pan American	-324	03/04/87	17/06/87	Clipper *Freedom*
443	9V-STP	Singapore Airlines	-324	02/10/87	22/12/88?	
444	C-FNWD	Wardair Canada	-304	26/10/87	22/12/87	*Jack Moar*
445	F-ODVF	Royal Jordanian	-304	09/11/87	08/02/88	*Princess Raiyah*
446	C-GBWD	Wardair Canada	-304	17/12/87	23/02/88	*C C Carl Agar*
447	C-GCWD	Wardair Canada	-304	20/01/88	20/03/88	*S R Stan Miller*
448	C-GDWD	Wardair Canada	-304	01/02/88	29/03/88	*T Rusty Blakey*
449	N813PA	Pan American	-324	07/05/87	19/07/87	Clipper *Great Republic* st Atlanta
450	N814PA	Pan American	-324	12/06/87	14/08/87	Clipper *Liberty Bell* w/o 31/03/95
451	N815PA	Pan American	-324	28/01/88	16/04/88	Clipper *Mayflower*
452	N816PA	Pan American	-324	21/07/87	30/09/87	Clipper *Meteor*
453	N817PA	Pan American	-324	11/08/87	15/10/87	Clipper *Midnight Sun*

Air India A310-300 in an experimental colour scheme.

C/N	Reg'n	Owner/operator	Model	First Flight	Delivery	Remarks
454	F-GEMG	Air France	-203	15/01/88	18/03/88	
455	N818PA	Pan American	-324	11/02/88	28/04/88	Clipper *Morning Star*
456	N819PA	Pan American	-324	04/03/88	28/05/88	Clipper *Northern Light*
457	N820PA	Pan American	-324	25/03/88	22/06/88	Clipper *Plymouth Rock*
458	N821PA	Pan American	-324	21/04/88	21/06/88	Clipper *Queen of the Skies*
467	N822PA	Pan American	-324	18/05/88	30/06/88	Clipper *Victory*
468	D-AHLZ	Hapag-Lloyd	-204	23/12/87	22/03/88	
472	C-GIWD	Wardair Canada	-304	07/03/88	19/05/88	*G W G Grant McConachie*
473	F-ODSV	Somali Airlines	-304	19/01/88	20/03/89	
		Air Algérie		ntu		
475	C-GJWD	Wardair Canada	-304	31/05/88	25/08/88	*Sheldon Luck*
476	TC-JCV	THY-Turkish Airlines	-304	27/01/88	11/04/88	*Aras*
478	TC-JCY	THY-Turkish Airlines	-304	25/02/88	15/06/88	*Coruh*
480	TC-JCZ	THY-Turkish Airlines	-304	06/04/88	22/06/88	*Ergene*
481	C-GKWD	Wardair Canada	-304	03/06/88	30/08/88	*W R Wop May*
482	C-GLWD	Wardair Canada	-304	13/07/88	29/09/88	*C H Punch Dickens*
483	CS-THE	TAP Air Portugal	-304	05/08/88	25/10/88	*Bartolomeu Dias*
484	D-AIDB	Lufthansa	-304	14/09/88	10/12/88	*Fürth*
485	D-AIDC	Condor	-304	14/09/88	02/11/88	
486	5B-DAX	Cyprus Airways	-204	05/10/88	28/02/89	*Engomi*
487	D-AHLX	Hapag-Lloyd	-204	02/11/88	30/12/88	
488	D-AIDD	Lufthansa	-304	13/01/89	08/03/89	*Emden*
489	OE-LAA	Austrian Airlines	-324	21/10/88	16/12/88	*New York*
490	F-ODVG	Royal Jordanian	-304	07/12/88	03/02/89	*Prince Faisal,*
	JY-CAG			ntu		
491	F-ODVH	Royal Jordanian	-304	04/01/89	15/03/89	*Prince Hamazeh,*
	JY-CAH			ntu		
492	OE-LAB	Austrian Airlines	-324	25/11/88	27/01/89	*Tokyo*
493	9V-STQ	Singapore Airlines	-324	09/01/89	07/03/89	
494	CS-TEJ	TAP Air Portugal	-304	09/11/88	01/03/89	Pedro Nunes
495	CS-TEI	TAP Air Portugal	-304	07/02/89	06/04/89	*Fernao de Magalhaes*
496	TC-JDA	THY-Turkish Airlines	-304	20/02/89	05/04/89	*Aksu*
497	TC-JDB	THY-Turkish Airlines	-304	08/03/89	28/04/89	*Goksu*
498	DDR-ABA	Interflug	-304	05/04/89	26/06/89	
	DDR-SZA			ntu		
499	DDR-ABB	Interflug	-304	20/04/89	30/06/89	
	DDR-SZB			ntu		
500	9V-STR	Singapore Airlines	-324	29/03/89	25/08/89	
501	9V-STS	Singapore Airlines	-324	12/04/89	29/09/89	
502	F-GEMN	Air France	-304	26/05/89	04/08/89	
	C-FZWD	Wardair		ntu		
503	DDR-ABC	Interflug	-304	29/06/89	23/10/89	
	DDR-SZC			ntu		
504	F-GEMO	Air France	-304	07/06/89	31/08/89	
	C-GPWD	Wardair		ntu		
519	5Y-BFT	Kenya Airways	-304	20/07/89	28/11/89	*Uhuru Star*
520	D-AHLA	Hapag-Lloyd	-304	05/07/89	09/10/89	
522	D-AIDE	Lufthansa	-304	25/08/89	27/10/89	*Speyer*
523	D-AIDI	Lufthansa	-304	13/09/89	02/03/90	*Fellbach*
524	D-AIDF	Lufthansa	-304	27/09/89	08/12/89	*Aschaffenburg*
526	D-AIDK	Lufthansa	-304	02/10/89	30/03/90	*Donaueschingen*

The A310-200 was operated in Thai Airways colours for only two years, before the domestic airline was merged into Thai International.

C/N	Reg'n	Owner/operator	Model	First Flight	Delivery	Remarks
527	D-AIDH	Lufthansa	-304	25/10/89	19/01/90	*Wetzlar*
528	D-AHLB	Hapag-Lloyd	-304	25/10/89	10/01/90	
531	F-ODVI	Royal Jordanian	-304	22/11/89	16/03/90	*Princess Haya*
534	9V-STT	Singapore Airlines	-324	01/12/89	13/02/90	
535	F-GHEJ	Air Liberté	-324	23/03/90	30/05/90	
537	TC-JDC	THY-Turkish Airlines	-304	19/01/90	27/03/90	*Meric*
538	VT-EQS	Air-India	-304	19/02/90	24/08/90	*Krishna*
539	N823PA	Pan American	-324	10/04/90	08/06/90	Clipper *Golden Light*
541	CS-TEW	TAP-Air Portugal	-304	13/03/90	10/05/90	
542	N824PA	Pan American	-324	24/04/90	26/06/90	Clipper *Golden Rule*
544	VT-EQT	Air-India	-304	18/06/90	30/08/90	*Narmada*
545	A6-EKG	Emirates Airlines	-304	04/07/90	03/01/92	
	F-GHEM	EAS		ntu		
547	D-AIDL	Lufthansa	-304	07/08/90	23/11/90	*Oberstdorf*
548	9V-STU	Singapore Airlines	-324	23/08/90	22/10/90	
549	P2-ANG	Air Nuigini	-324	07/09/90	21/12/90	
550	F-GEMP	Air France	-304	25/09/90	10/12/90	
551	F-GEMQ	Air France	-304	29/10/90	12/02/91	
552	F-GKTD	Trans European (TEA)	-304	19/10/90	19/12/90	
562	F-GKTE	Trans European (TEA)	-307	09/11/90	20/03/91	
564	OK-WAA	CSA-Czechoslovak A/L	-304	22/11/90	11/02/91	*Praha*
565	CS-TEX	TAP-Air Portugal	-304	12/12/90	06/03/91	*Joao XXI*
567	OK-WAB	CSA	-304	03/01/91	12/03/91	*Bratislava*
568	OE-LAC	Austrian Airlines	-324ET	23/01/91	26/03/91	*Paris*
570	9V-STV	Singapore Airlines	-324	30/01/91	29/03/91	
571	TU-TAC	Air Afrique	-304	07/02/91	29/04/91	
	F-GHYM	EAS		ntu		
573	CS-TEY	TAP-Air Portugal	-304	22/02/91	07/05/91	*Pedro Alvares Cabral*
574	HC-BRA	Ecuatoriana	-324	01/03/91	26/09/91	*Cuidad de Guayaquil*
576	HC-BRB	Ecuatoriana	-324	20/03/91	27/09/91	*Ciudad de Quito*
585	AP-BDZ	Pakistan International	-308	18/03/91	25/06/91	
586	TC-JDD	THY-Turkish Airlines	-304	29/03/91	11/07/91	*Dalaman*
587	AP-BEB	Pakistan International	-308	15/05/91	26/07/91	
588	A6-EKI	Emirates Airline	-308	23/05/91	29/07/92	
	I-TEAB	TEA Italy		ntu		
589	9V-STW	Singapore Airlines	-324	15/05/91	24/07/91	
590	AP-BEC	Pakistan International	-308	03/06/91	02/09/91	
591	HS-TYQ	Royal Thai Air Force	-324	11/06/91	05/11/91	
592	F-OGQQ	Aeroflot	-308	22/07/91	12/08/92	*Tschaikovski*
593	F-OGQR	Aeroflot	-308	02/08/91	27/08/92	*Rachmaninov*
594	VR-BMU	Aerocancun	-324	01/08/91	13/12/91	*Baleares*
595	D-AIDM	Lufthansa	-304	30/08/91	08/11/91	*Chemnitz*
596	F-OGQS	Aeroflot	-308	11/09/91	11/12/92	*Glinka*, w/o 23/03/94
597	A6-EKJ	Emirates Airline	-308	24/09/91	07/08/92	
		TEA		ntu		
598	HC-BRP	SAETA Ecuador	-304	31/10/91	16/03/92	*Galapagos*
599	D-AIDN	Lufthansa	-304	16/10/91	10/02/92	*Gütersloh*
600	A6-EKH	Emirates Airline	-308	04/11/91	26/02/92	
620	D-AHLC	Hapag-Lloyd	-308	08/11/91	31/01/92	
622	F-OGQT	Aeroflot	-308	02/12/91	30/07/92	*Moussorgski*
624	OE-LAD	Austrian Airlines	-325	06/12/91	09/03/92	*Chicago*
634	9V-STX	Singapore Airlines	-324	18/12/91	28/02/92	
636	YR-LCA	Tarom Romanian Airlines	-325	13/01/92	17/12/92	*Transylvania*
638	EC-117	Oasis Airlines	-324	27/01/92	15/04/92	

C/N	Reg'n	Owner/operator	Model	First Flight	Delivery	Remarks
640	HB-IPL	Balair	-325	06/02/92	27/04/92	
642	HB-IPM	Balair	-325ET	20/02/92	30/04/92	
644	YR-LCB	Tarom	-325	09/03/92	17/12/92	*Moldova*
646	F-OGQU	Aeroflot	-308	19/03/92	30/06/92	*Skriabin*
647	9K-ALA	Kuwait Airways	-308	28/10/92	19/05/93	*Al-Ghara*
648	9K-ALD	Kuwait Government	-308	06/04/92	02/11/93	
		TEA		ntu		
649	9K-ALB	Kuwait Airways	-308	05/10/92	18/06/93	*Ghamada*
650	N835AB	Delta Air Lines	-324	24/04/92	31/03/93	st Atlanta
651	TU-TAD	Air Afrique	-308	20/05/92	12/08/92	
652	TU-TAE	Air Afrique	-308	27/05/92	04/09/92	
653	AP-BEG	Pakistan International	-308	25/06/92	23/09/92	
654	9V-STZ	Singapore Airlines	-324	25/06/92	25/09/92	
		TEA		ntu		
656	AP-BEQ	Pakistan International	-308	07/92	21/12/93	
		LACSA		ntu		
658	A6-EKK	Emirates Airline	-308	03/09/92	19/11/92	
660	N836AB	Delta Air Lines	-324	16/10/92	30/09/93	
661	HC-BSF	SAETA Ecuador	-304	03/11/92	22/01/93	*Guayas*
663	9K-ALC	Kuwait Airways	-308	17/11/92	30/06/93	*Kadhma*
665	9V-STA	Singapore Airlines	-324	09/12/92	19/03/93	
667	A6-EKL	Emirates Airline	-308	11/01/93	30/03/93	
669	9V-STB	Singapore Airlines	-324	01/02/93	23/04/93	
671	TU-TAF	Air Afrique	-308	19/02/93	11/08/93	
672	HB-IPN	Balair CTA	-325	24/02/93	19/05/93	
674	N837AB	Delta Air Lines	-324	17/03/93	27/07/93	st Atlanta
676	N838AB	Delta Air Lines	-324	29/04/93	15/09/93	st Atlanta
678	N839AB	Delta Air Lines	-324	28/05/93	05/11/93	
680	9V-STC	Singapore Air Lines	-324	10/06/93	09/09/93	
682	N840AB	Delta Air Lines	-324	24/06 or 07/93	19/11/93	
684	9V-STD	Singapore Airlines	-324	19/08/93	28/10/93	
686	N841AB	Delta Air Lines	-324	27/08/93	01/12/93	
687	N842AB	Delta Air Lines	-324	13/09/93	22/12/93	
689	N843AB	Delta Air Lines	-324	28/09/93	29/12/93	st Atlanta
691	AP-BEU	Pakistan International	-308	08/02/94	11/05/94	
693	9V-STE	Singapore Airlines	-324	17/06/94	17/06/94	
695	A6-EKP	Emirates Airline	-308	08/11/94	15/05/95	
697	9V-STF	Singapore Airlines	-324	18/01/95	16/03/95	
698	S2-ADE	Bangladesh Biman	-325	13/06/96		*City of Hazrat Khan Jahan Ali (RA)*
700	S2-ADF	Bangladesh Biman	-325	19/08/96		*City of Chittagong*
702	F-OHPR	Yemenia	-325	20/01/97	18/03/97	
704	F-OHPS	Yemenia	-325	04/02/97	28/03/97	

OVER PAGE: A310-300 protoype touching down at Toulouse.

8 CHRONOLOGY

The idea of international collaboration and joint development of aircraft was discussed long before the thinking crystallised towards an Airbus. People involved in these exchanges of opinions included Thalau, Valière, Dr Weinhart, Ziegler and Salvador.

June 1965 Initial talks begin between the German and French aircraft industry on the occasion of the Paris Air Show. Participants are Dr Weinhardt, L Bölkow and General Puget

2 July 1965 Airbus study group is established in Munich with the aim of undertaking preparatory work for international co-operation

6 August 1965 Deutsche Airbus holds discussions with the Lufthansa executive board on the design of the aircraft, but finds the German flag-carrier unenthusiastic

22 October 1965 British European Airways (BEA)-led symposium in London brings together Europe's major airlines. Varied reactions to the Airbus concept, but generally negative

22 December 1965 British transport minister visits Bonn and requests the Federal government to participate in a trilateral development of the Airbus. Jenkins agrees to try and persuade France to take a similar line. As a result, Germany's economics minister Schmücker agrees to a 25 percent participation.

23 December 1965 Joint-venture team Airbus is founded in Germany tasked with presenting a German project to the Federal Ministry of Economics

January 1966 First negotiations on the design of the Airbus are held by the joint-venture team

4 February 1966 Deutsche Airbus visits Fokker in the Netherlands, which considers design too large

9 March 1966 First trilateral government meeting concerning the technical design. Britain and France were in favour of a twin-engined aircraft for 180 passengers, while Germany preferred 250-300 passengers and four engines

23 March 1996 Government meeting in Munich fails to agree on technical design. Market analysis is considered wrong

11 May 1966 Similar government meeting in London also ends without agreement, but concession on number of passengers made in follow-up meeting nine days later

14 June 1966 At another meeting in London, Britain suggests that its participation depends on the selection of the Rolls-Royce RB.207 power plant

8 September 1966 First official consultation takes place between the companies in Germany, France and Great Britain at Hawker Siddeley, on the occasion of the Farnborough Air Show. Britain and France are of the opinion that the time had come for the aircraft industry in the three countries to take the lead, as almost a year had been lost through protracted negotiations at government level. The meeting lays the foundations for all future industry meetings

21 September 1966 Top level industry meeting in Paris discusses the preparation of joint proposals to be submitted to the three governments, providing evidence of the viability of the Airbus project

15 October 1966 Joint proposals and applications for financial participation are presented to the three governments

6 March 1967 Government meeting in London decision is made in favour of Rolls-Royce RB.207-3 engines

9 May 1967 After several postponements of a decision, a trilateral ministerial meeting in Paris approves the undertaking. The industry is requested to supply a joint study by 30 June for an Airbus with two RB.207 engines

25 July 1967 Trilateral government decision is made regarding the start of the definition phase

4 September 1967 Deutsche Airbus grouping is registered in Munich, comprising Dornier, Hamburger Flugzeugbau (HFB), Messerschmitt-Werke Flugzeug-Union-Süd, Siebelwerke and Vereinigte Flugtechnische Werke (VFW). Each company contributes DM1 million to the DM5 million registered capital

September 1967 Airbus contract is signed by the governments of Germany, France and Great Britain

August 1968 Final decision is postponed until November

11 December 1968 Decision is made to build a smaller version, first designated A250, then A300B

February 1969 Federal government decides to continue its support for the Airbus project, even if Britain should withdraw

ABOVE: The extended-range A310-300 became the most popular of the family.

March 1969 French government announces that Airbus would be built under any circumstances

10 April 1969 British government withdraws amid doubts over the viability of the project

29 May 1969 Airbus development contract is signed by German economics Minister Karl Schiller and French Transport Minister M Jean Chamont at Le Bourget, on the opening of the Paris Air Show

18 December 1970 Establishment of Airbus Industrie, a Groupe d'Interets Economique (GIE) in Paris

28 December 1970 Fokker-VFW joins Airbus Industrie

27 May- Mock-up of the A300 is presented at the 29th Paris
6 June 1971 Air Show at Le Bourget

9 November 1971 Air France becomes first Airbus customer, with a firm contract for six A300B2, plus 10 options

21 December 1971 Contract is signed by the Banque Européenne d'Investissements and Aerospatiale for the investment necessary to finance the construction of the prototype Airbus A300B

23 December 1971 The foreign minister of Spain and the ambassadors of France and Germany sign accord for Spain's participation on the A300 programme

28 September 1972 The first Airbus A300 prototype is rolled out at Toulouse, in a joint presentation with the pre-production Anglo-French Concorde supersonic airliner

28 October 1972 Airbus A300B1 takes off on its maiden flight from Toulouse, one month ahead of schedule

15 March 1974 The Airbus A300B2 receives its certification from the French and German authorities.

30 May 1974 Airbus receives US certification from the Federal Aviation Administration (FAA)

30 September 1974 Airbus receives Cat IIIa autoland certification

26 December 1974 Increased-range A300B4 (aircraft No.9) makes its maiden flight

February 1975 Bernard Lathiere is nominated president and chief executive of Airbus Industrie

26 March 1975 A300B4 receives certification

6 July 1978 Swissair and Lufthansa sign Memorandum of Understanding (MoU) for the acquisition of the A300B10 (later re-designated A300-10 and then A310), effectively launching this new type

18 August 1978 The Airbus Industrie partners and British Aerospace initial agreement for BAe's entry as a full partner

29 November 1978 BAe's full partnership agreement receives official signature. The British company takes 20 percent stake in Airbus Industrie with effect from 1 January 1979

15 March 1979 Swissair places firm order for 10 A310-200 and takes options on a further 10 of the same type

31 March 1979 West African multi-national carrier Air Afrique signs up for two A310-300, together with one A300B4-200

2 April 1979 German flag-carrier Lufthansa orders 25 A310, plus 25 options: including the conversion of nine A300 options

3 April 1979 KLM Royal Dutch Airlines signs firm purchase contract for 10 A310-200

6 April 1979 Airbus Industrie signs agreement with Belairbus of Belgium to participate as a subcontractor

10 April 1979 British low-fare charter carrier Laker Airways orders 10 A300B4-200, with the option to convert the final two aircraft to the A310

9 May 1979 Air France agrees to buy 15 A310-200, including five firm and 10 options

11 June 1979 Agreement is reached between Airbus Industrie and Rolls-Royce

29 October 1979 British Caledonian Airways sign MoU for the acquisition of six A310-200, split equally between firm orders and options

30 October 1979 Martinair Holland places firm order for three A310-200s and one option. Order includes one passenger aircraft and two A310-200C Combis

31 October 1979 Sabena becomes last major European flag-carrier to sign for Airbus, ordering three A310-200, plus three options

27 December 1979 Yugoslavian airline Inex Adria (now independent Slovenia's Adria Airways) orders four A310, including two firm and two options

31 January 1980 British Caledonian Airways converts its MoU of 29 October 1979 into a firm contract

28 May 1980 Austrian Airlines becomes another new Airbus customer with an order for two A310-200, plus an equal number of options

27 June 1980 Kuwait Airways announces intention to order six A310-200, increasing it to 11 on 25 September

4 December 1980 Air France signs order announced on 9 May 1979

6 December 1980 Kuwait Airways signs contract for six A310-200 and takes five options

1 January 1981 Inex Adria cancels its Airbus order signed on 27 December 1979

27 February 1981 Air Afrique converts its two A310 orders into A300B4

28 February 1981 Cruzeiro do Sul drops two A310 options

25 March 1981 Canada's largest charter airline Wardair Canada signs firm contract for six A310-200, plus six options

17 April 1981 Nigeria Airways places firm order for four A310-200 and takes out a similar number of options

15 September 1981 Libyan Arab Airlines orders four A310-200, together with A300B4-200 and two A300C4-200

30 September 1981 Singapore Airlines converts options for six A300B4-200 into firm orders and takes options on two A310-200

30 October 1981 Middle East Airlines Airliban signs contract for five A310-200 and options 14 more

16 February 1982 Roll-out ceremony takes place at Toulouse of first Airbus A310

25 February 1982 Cyprus Airways orders four A310-200, made up of two firm and two options

3 April 1982 Airbus A310-200 makes 3 hour 15 minute maiden flight, piloted by Bernard Ziegler and Pierre Baud

11 June 1982 Sudan Airways contracts to buy three new A310, but operates only second-hand models

21 July 1982 Brazilian airline VASP signs for nine Pratt & Whitney-powered A310-200

11 March 1983 A310 receives type certification from the French and German airworthiness authorities

29 March 1983 Swissair and Lufthansa take simultaneous delivery of the first A310s. Swissair also announces intention to change four of its order to the extended-range A310-300 variant

April 1983 Lufthansa inaugurates the first A310 service

31 May 1983 Singapore Airlines places firm order for six -200s

28 September 1983 A310 receives French and German certification to JAR Cat IIIA automatic landing capability

January 1984 A310 obtains UK certification

25 May 1984 Pan Am places order for 12 A310-300, plus 13 options. Also acquires four A310-200 on interim basis

30 May 1984 Air Algerié signs up for two A310-200

25 November 1984 Martinair Holland takes delivery of first convertible A310-200C

28 November 1984 A310 receives JAR certification for Cat IIIb automatic landing

8 December 1984 Turkish Airlines-THY orders 14 A310-200, including seven firm and seven options

1985 A310 obtains FAA type approval

29 March 1985 Thai Airways orders two A310-200 for domestic trunk routes

1 April 1985 Jean Pierson takes over as MD from Roger Beteille

8 April 1985 Air-India orders six A310-300

16 April 1985 The CAA of China orders three A310-200, and follows up on 7 May 1986 for two A310-300

8 July 1985 Extended-range A310-300, powered by two Pratt & Whitney JT9D-7R4E engines, takes off on its maiden flight

6 September 1985 First A310-300 with General Electric CF6-80C2 engines makes first flight

8 October 1985 Kenya Airways becomes first customer for the A310-300 in Africa, signing for two A310-300. Air Afrique had placed earlier order, but this was changed to the A300

5 December 1985 A310-300 receives type approval from French and German authorities

17 December 1985 Launch customer Swissair accepts delivery of first A310-300

April 1986 General-Electric CF6-80C2-powered A310-300 obtains certification

April 1986 First A310-300 with General Electric engines is delivered to Air-India

29 April 1986 Thai Airways takes delivery of first A310-200 with newly introduced wingtip fences

9 May 1986 Royal Jordanian orders six -300s (plus six A320)

23 October 1986 Emirates places order for two General Electric-powered A310-300

June 1987 A310-300 obtains certification with Pratt & Whitney PW4152 Engines

17 June 1987 Pan Am takes delivery of first PW4152-powered A310-300

15 October 1987 Somali Airlines becomes new Airbus customer with order for one A310-300 and one option

7 June 1988 Interflug becomes first carrier from the Soviet Bloc with a contract for three A310-300

22 February 1988 TAP Air Portugal signs contract for two A310-300

3 October 1988 Airbus Industrie chairman Dr Franz Josef Strauss dies

17 November 1988 Dr Hans Friderichs is elected chairman of the Airbus Industrie Supervisory Board

28 April 1989 Belgian charter airline Trans European Airways (TEA) places order for eight A310-300

8 August 1989 Pakistan International Airlines contracts to buy three A310-300 and takes options on three more

9 September 1989 Oasis International orders four A310-300 for use by its Mexican subsidiary Aerocancun

24 September 1991 Ecuatoriana orders its first Airbus, signing up for two A310-300 powered by PW4152 turbofan engines

30 June 1992 Aeroflot takes delivery of first of five new A310-300

1 April 1994 Daimler-Benz Chairman Edzard Reuter replaces Dr Hans Friderichs as Chairman of the Supervisory Board

31 January 1995 Biman Bangladesh orders two PW4000-powered A310-300

31 December 1995 Yemenia-Yemen Airways Corporation is the latest Middle East airline to opt for Airbus, ordering two A310-300

1996 PW4000-powered A310 receives cold weather certification (down to -54°C) from the Interstate Aviation Committee-Aviation Register (IAC-AR) of the Russian Federation and Associated States

13 January 1997 Airbus partners sign a memorandum of understanding (MoU) to restructure Airbus Industrie into a limited liability company by 1999

27 June 1997 Former President and Chief Operating Officer Bernard Lathière dies suddenly at the age of 68.

1 April 1998 Noel Forgeard takes over as Managing Director from Jean Pierson, and Manfred Bischoff succeeds Edzard Reuter as Chairman of the Supervisory Board

15 June 1998 Uzbekistan Airways takes delivery of last A310-300 built to date

23 July 1998 An era ends with the death of Airbus Industrie's first President Henri Ziegler

INDEX